National Trust Walks

2. Southern and central Wales

National Trust Walks

Walks

2. Southern and Central Wales

Dorothy Hamilton

DOROTHY HAMILTON

Dorothy lives in Meirionnydd. She has written other walking guide-books, including Circular Walks on Anglesey, Circular Walks in Meirionnydd, Circular Walks Around Beddgelert, Circular Walks in the Vale of Glamorgan and Walks from Welsh Heritage Railways. She also writes for walking and history magazines. A keen walker, she has undertaken several long distance walks in Wales, Scotland, England, Eire, Norway, France and other European countries.

First published in 2007

© Text: Dorothy Hamilton
© Photographs: Dorothy Hamilton/Gwasg Carreg Gwalch

ISBN: 1-84524-076-6
978-1-84524-076-9

Published by
Llygad Gwalch,
Ysgubor Plas, Llwyndyrys, Pwllheli, Gwynedd, Wales, LL53 6NG.
Tel: 01758 750432
e-mail: gai@llygadgwalch.com
www.llygadgwalch.com

Introduction

With the publication of this book, the National Trust marks another important landmark in its history. Without doubt, one of the best ways to appreciate our houses and landscapes is to visit them on foot, to admire them at leisure and savour their unique atmosphere.

The number of National Trust properties has increased over the years, especially in rural areas and it is more important now than ever to ensure rural communities enjoy a prosperous future by safeguarding what is currently in place, and supporting suitable developments for the future. This can be achieved by working with a number of agencies on a national level but also through creative initiatives, such as the publication of this book, which will enable ramblers to enjoy the countryside and take pleasure from the warm welcome and hospitality offered to them by local people.

The National Trust is not just a guardian of historic houses; it is an organisation which protects a substantial part of Wales' mountains, valleys, beaches and coastlines. The public have been generous in their support of appeals for money and as a result the National Trust's property portfolio has increased dramatically. One example of this is the Neptune Coastline Campaign, launched forty-one years ago in a bid to buy parts of coastline under threat. As a direct result of this appeal, the National Trust now protects 140 miles of beautiful coastline and beaches which are free from any unsuitable commercial threat and available for all to enjoy.

The land and properties under the National Trust's protection are among our greatest national assets. They include open spaces as well as buildings, which show clearly how man's love for his home, be it a palace or a cottage has evolved over the course of time. Needless to say, these are beautiful places to behold but the

National Trust is aware of the need to take further steps. Every effort is now made to explain how our environment originated and evolved, whether it be natural or of man's making. It is imperative that we can interpret and understand our past and present before we can lay firm foundations for the future.

And that is the great benefit of this book. By leading us to so many of the National Trust's treasures, we are given a remarkable and revealing glimpse of Welsh landscape, heritage and culture.

Iwan Huws, Director of the National Trust in Wales

Using this Guidebook

The walks in this book are circular routes, and they range in length from three and a half miles to ten miles. All start at or near parking places, and most of them are on bus routes. Bus timetables are available from Tourist Information Centres. Some of the National Trust properties are closed in the winter, or on certain days of the week, therefore it is advisable to check opening times before starting out. Phone numbers are given under the name of the property where applicable.

Places of historical interest are printed in bold in the directions, and information about them is at the end of each walk. Adequate route directions are given to follow the walks without referring to detailed maps, but if you prefer to carry one, the relevant OS Explorer map is listed on the Contents page.

Some of the walks pass refreshment places on the route, but for the longer walks it is advisable to carry food and drink for snacks along the way. All the walks require sturdy footwear, and it is usually a good idea to carry waterproofs.

THE COUNTRY CODE
Guard against any risk of fire.
Keep to the public rights of way when crossing farmland.
Avoid causing any damage to walls, fences and hedges.
Leave farm gates as you find them.
Keep dogs under control and on leads in the presence of livestock.
Leave machinery, farm animals and crops alone.
Take care not to pollute water.
Carry your litter home with you.
Protect all wildlife, plants and trees.
Avoid making any unnecessary noise.
Drive carefully on country roads.
Enjoy and respect the countryside.

PLACE-NAMES

The following words are sometimes used in the names of places in Wales. They may be followed by the name of a saint or a topographical feature such as a river.

Aber – *estuary, river mouth*
Afon – *river*
Allt/Gallt – *hill, slope*
Bach/Fach – *small*
Bedd – *grave, tomb*
Beudy – *cow shed*
Braich – *arm*
Bryn – *hill*
Bwlch – *pass*
Bychan – *little*
Cadair/Gadair – *chair*
Cae – *field*
Caer/Gaer – *fort*
Canol – *middle, centre*
Capel – *chapel*
Carn – *cairn*
Carreg – *rock, stone*
Castell – *castle*
Cefn – *ridge*
Celyn – *holly*
Cloch – *bell*
Clogwyn – *cliff, ridge*
Coch – *red*
Coed – *wood, trees*
Craig – *rock*
Croes – *cross*
Cwm – *valley*
Dinas – *fort*
Dôl/Ddôl – *meadow*
Drws – *door*
Du/Ddu – *black*

Dŵr – *water*
Dyffryn – *valley, vale*
Eglwys – *church*
Esgob – *bishop*
Ffordd – *road*
Ffridd – *mountain pasture*
Ffynnon – *spring, well*
Garth – *hill, enclosure*
Glan – *riverbank*
Glas – *blue*
Glyn – *glen, valley*
Golau – *light*
Gorsaf – *station*
Gwaun/Waun – *moor*
Gwern – *swamp, alder trees*
Gwyn – *white*
Hafod/Hafoty – *summer dwelling*
Hen – *old*
Hendre – *winter dwelling*
Heol – *road*
Isaf – *lower*
Lôn – *lane*
Llan – *church*
Llety – *lodging*
Llwybr – *path*
Llwyn – *grove*
Llyn – *lake*
Llys – *court, palace*
Maen – *stone*
Maes – *field*

Mawr/Fawr – *big, great*
Melin/Felin – *mill*
Moel/Foel – *mountain*
Môr – *sea*
Morfa – *marsh*
Muriau – *walls*
Mynydd/Fynydd – *mountain*
Nant – *stream, ravine*
Neuadd – *hall*
Newydd – *new*
Ogof – *cave*
Pandy – *fulling-mill*
Pant – *hollow, valley*
Parc – *park, field*
Pen – *head, top*
Penrhyn – *promontory, headland*
Pentir – *headland*
Pentre – *village*
Pistyll – *spout, cataract*
Plas – *mansion*
Pont – *bridge*
Porth – *port*
Pwll – *pool*
Rhaeadr – *cataract, waterfall*
Rhos – *moorland, heath*
Rhyd – *ford*
Sarn – *causeway, road*
Tafarn – *inn*
Tal – *tall, high*
Tan – *under*
Traeth – *beach*
Tre/Tref – *town*
Trwyn – *promontory*
Twr – *tower*
Tŷ – *house*
Tyddyn – *smallholding, small farm*

Uchaf – *upper*
Y/Yr – *the*
Ynys – *island*

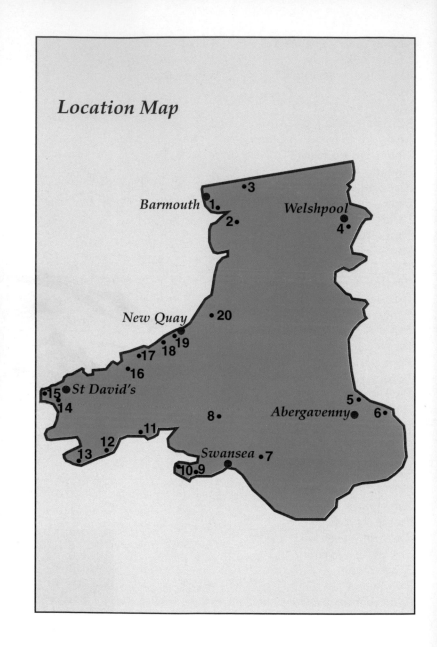

Location Map

Barmouth 1.
•3
2•
Welshpool
4•

New Quay •20

•19
17• 18•
•16
15• • St David's
14•
5•
8• Abergavenny 6•
11•
12•
13•
Swansea •7
10• •9

The Routes

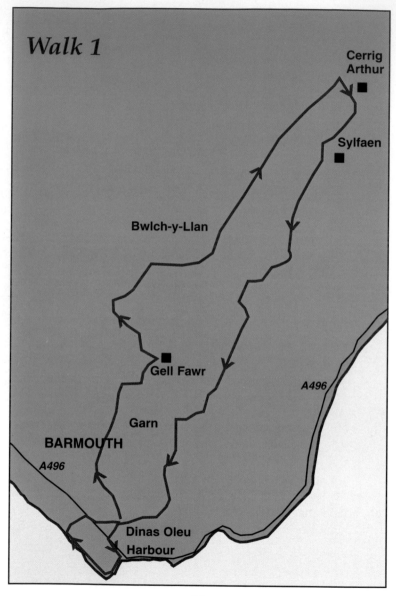

Walk 1

Cerrig Arthur

Sylfaen

Bwlch-y-Llan

Gell Fawr

A496

Garn

BARMOUTH

A496

Dinas Oleu

Harbour

14

I. Diпas Olev

Dinas Oleu, 'The Fortress of Light', was the first property to be given to the National Trust. The gorse covered hillside was donated by Mrs Fanny Talbot on the 29th of March 1895. A wealthy philanthropist, she lived at Ty'n y Ffynnon, a villa on the hillside near Dinas Oleu. She was a friend of Octavia Hill and Canon Hardwick Rawnsley, two founders of the National Trust, and she wished to secure for the public the enjoyment of the hill for ever, without the risk of it being disfigured.

Tŷ Crwn, Barmouth

The original piece of land was less than five acres, but since then another 13 acres have been added. A seat and viewpoint, in the shape of a C, was erected at the top of Dinas Oleu in 1995 to mark the centenary of the gift to the National Trust. From the hill are splendid views of Abermaw (Barmouth), Afon Mawddach estuary and Cardigan Bay, with the Llŷn peninsula and Ynys Enlli (Bardsey Island) to the north.

The walk – *after climbing to Dinas Oleu, the route makes a gradual ascent to Bwlch y Llan and proceeds to a prehistoric stone circle before returning to Barmouth along lanes and paths offering stunning views of Afon Mawddach and the Cader Idris range.*
7 miles – about 4 hours

Afon Mawddach

Centenary Seat

Park your car at **Barmouth** main car park (opposite the beach). If travelling by public transport, you can join the route near the start, at the level crossing close to Barmouth railway station and bus terminus.

On leaving the car park, bear right to have the beach on your left. Pass the Lifeboat Station and the Leisure Centre, then bear right and cross the level crossing and Jubilee Road. Walk ahead to the main road and turn right to cross the road at the pedestrian crossing. Bear right and in a few paces go left up Dinas Olau Road. Cross over a narrow road and walk up a steep hill which soon bears right. On reaching a fork, take the right-hand lane and, shortly, take a path on the left. After passing a house on the left, go left up steps and bear left to a National Trust information board. On your right is the gorse covered hill, Dinas Oleu.

Take a winding path uphill through the gorse and go right at a fork. A few paces before reaching a gate in the upper wall, bear left on a path. Join another path and bear right uphill, soon winding left to reach the commemorative seat on Dinas Oleu.

From the seat, go through a gate in the wall above it and walk uphill to join a path. Turn left to go through a gate in a wall, and follow the path downhill to a wider path. Turn right uphill and, after going through a gate, you will reach the buildings of the derelict farm, Cell-fechan. Ignore a gap into a field on your left and continue uphill. Ignore another gap on the left, but go through the next gap to have a wall on your left and another closeby on your right. Continue beside the left-hand wall. The path bends right to pass above a little valley, and goes through a gate. After a few paces, go left on a path through rushes to a small slab bridge over a stream, and a small gate. Continue beside a right-hand fence and follow it around a bend to pass a barn on your left, and reach a track at the house called Gellfawr.

Turn left on a clear track and pass buildings. The track goes uphill through gorse then bends left between walls to pass

Cerrig Arthur Stone Circle

above a ruin. Ignore a gate on the left and walk on beside a fence to a ladder stile and gate. Continue on the clear track, with good views of the coastline and Cardigan Bay and, when the left-hand wall veers left, follow the grassy track ahead to a track junction. Turn left and walk downhill to climb a stile near a gate. Immediately bear right and go uphill to follow a clear path through **Bwlch y Llan.**

Higher up the pass you will have a wall on your right, but the path soon veers left away from it. Ignore a path on the right to a gate (unless you need an escape route, it joins the walk near a mast). Further on, continue beside the wall and, after climbing a stile near a gate, you will have open views across Afon Mawddach. Follow a gently descending track to another stile and continue across the open hillside. Cross a small stream and go through a gate at sheepfolds. Pass a ruin on your right and veer slightly right to go through a gate in the right-hand corner. In front of you, slightly left, is the **Cerrig Arthur** stone circle.

Bear right and, after joining a lower track, go through a gate on your right. Pass buildings at Sylfaen and turn right along a lane. Pass houses and turn right on a path that rises between walls to a stile and gate. Walk uphill and go through a gap. Have a wall on your left and the mast on your right but, before reaching a gap in the wall ahead, veer right to have another wall on your left. Pass the mast and small buildings on your right and go through a gate in the wall in front of you.

Turn left beside the wall to a ladder stile, and bear left. The path soon veers right through a gap in a wall and, further on, has a wall on the left. After passing through a gap in the wall ahead, more views open up of Afon Mawddach. The path goes along a little ridge, then veers right to cross a small stream and continues downhill to a gate and lane. Turn right to a stile at a gate and walk uphill.

A few paces before the lane bears right, go left to follow a path that passes below rock slabs. The path goes downhill and, eventually, after passing through two gates, reaches a small gate in the right-hand wall. Go through it to follow a narrow path through gorse and join another path near a seat and wall. Bear right and follow the path alongside the left-hand wall to a small gate signed **Frenchman's Grave Only.**

After viewing the grave, continue along the path and, after going through a gate in a wall, you will rejoin you outward route on Dinas Oleu. Walk downhill to the lane and turn left, soon bearing right on the path used earlier. After a few paces, at the path junction, bear left, then right down steps. After passing houses, turn right and keep right at the next junction to walk down steps to a lane. Descend more steps to reach the main road in Abermaw.

Turn left and after passing St David's Church bear right at the harbour. On your left, protected by low railings, is the sculpture called **The Last Haul.** Follow the pavement beside the harbour, to have fine views of **Pont y Bermo.** On your right is **Tŷ Gwyn** and, behind it, **Tŷ Crwn** (Round House). A few more minutes walk will bring you to the start of the walk at the car park and beach.

OTHER POINTS OF INTEREST
Barmouth. Where the streets of Barmouth are now was once the

Afon Mawddach estuary

Tŷ Gwyn

river's estuary. In 1565 there were only four houses and a couple of ferries. The development of the place as a port was mainly due to the growth of the wool industry in Meirionnydd. The hillsides beside Afon Mawddach were clothed in oak forests and between 1750 and 1865 more than 300 ships were built on its shores. Meanwhile Barmouth had become known for its sea bathing and the first hotel, Corsygedol,was built in 1795. The oldest houses in the town are those built on the cliff face. Sandbanks eventually blocked the original entrance to the river, and the High Street was built in the early 19th century. The coming of the railway brought even more visitors to this charming little resort situated at the mouth of one of the most beautiful estuaries in Wales.

Bwlch y Llan. On Boxing Day 1943, an Avro Anson flew into the hillside at Bwlch y Llan in low cloud, whilst returning to base at RAF Llandwrog after a routine navigational exercise. None of the four crew survived.

Cerrig Arthur Stone Circle. Only a few stones remain standing from this badly damaged circle, which lies at the junction of two ancient tracks. Some stumps can be seen partly covered with grass. The tall stones could be the entrance to a burial chamber.

The Frenchman's Grave. The Frenchman, Auguste Guyard, had tried unsuccessfully to set up a community in France. He eventually came to Wales and lived in one of the cottages Mrs Talbot had given to writer and socialist John Ruskin, who was experimenting with social living through his organization the Guild of St George. Guyard taught his neighbours how to grow vegetables and herbs, and the use of medicinal plants. He died in 1883 and his burial place is a walled plot overlooking the harbour.

The Last Haul. The sculpture of three fishermen hauling a net was made from a block of marble recovered from an 18th century shipwreck a few miles north along the Meirionnydd coast. The wreck is thought to have been a galleon from Genoa, northern Italy, which ran into a terrific storm on its way to an

Barmouth beach

unknown destination. The Last Haul was made by local sculptor Frank Cocksey. An exhibition about the shipwreck can be seen in Tŷ Gwyn.

Pont y Bermo. The railway bridge that spans Afon Mawddach estuary is nearly half a mile long. Before the building of the bridge, travellers had to cross the estuary by ferry, often in choppy seas. After the railway had reached the Cambrian coast, work soon started on bridging the estuary. During excavations for the foundations it was found that the rock floor was 120 feet below the alluvial deposits, and the iron pillars had to be sunk to this level to ensure that they stood on solid rock. Originally, when the bridge opened in 1867, it had a drawbridge section to allow the passage of tall ships. It was replaced in 1900 by a swing bridge. In the 1980s some of the timber piles had to be replaced when it was discovered they were being attacked by marine boring worms.

Tŷ Gwyn. This medieval building was built by Gruffudd

Fychan (Vaughan) of Corsygedol during the Wars of the Roses. He was a Lancastrian supporter and the house was a safe, secret meeting place. It is said that Jasper Tudor, the Earl of Pembroke and uncle to the future Henry V11, plotted with his supporters here to overthrow Richard 111 and put Henry V11 on the throne. The upper floor is now a museum, open in the summer months. **Tŷ Crwn.** The Round House was erected in 1834 to lock up drunken sailors and

The Last Haul

other disorderly people until they were sober enough to appear in court. The walls are two feet thick and the building is divided into two cells, one for men and one for women. It was only in use until 1861, but has been restored.

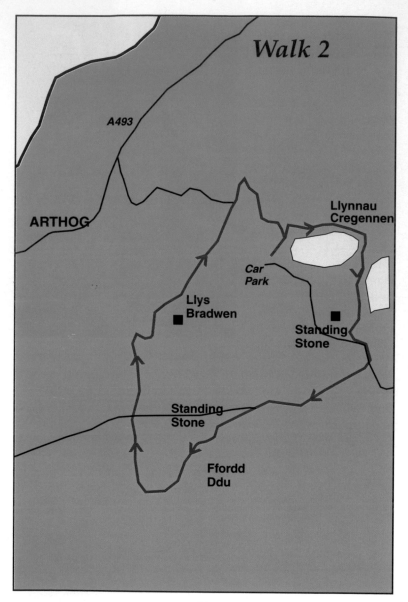

Walk 2

A493

ARTHOG

Llynnau
Cregennen

Car
Park

Llys
Bradwen

Standing
Stone

Standing
Stone

Ffordd
Ddu

2. Llynnau Cregennen

Afon Mawddach estuary

Llynnau Cregennen have been in the care of the National Trust since 1959. They were given by Major Wynne Jones in memory of his two sons who were killed during the second World War. Above the beautiful lakes towers Pared y Cefn Hir with its Iron Age hill fort. A number of standing stones will be seen during the walk. They are thought to be Bronze Age marker stones that were set alongside prehistoric routes through the mountains.

The walk – *after following paths beside the two lakes, the walk continues through moorland and pasture offering superb views of Afon Mawddach estuary.*
5 miles – about 3 hours

Start at the car park beside Llynnau Cregennen. It can be reached from a lane off the A493, north-west of Fairbourne and

Bridge over Afon Arthog

near Arthog, or from Dolgellau. The nearest bus stop is at Arthog, one mile off-route.

From the car park, walk out to the lane and turn left to have the lake on your right. After 200 metres, bear right at a footpath signpost and climb a ladder stile in a wall. Ignore a path on the left in the direction of Pared y Cefn Hir and walk ahead through the heather. Have the lake on your right but, when it curves to the right, continue along the main path and, after about 100 metres, bear right at a post with a green arrow. Pass another waymarked post and go over a slight rise to a corner of the lake.

Walk on beside the lake and cross a small bridge. Ignore a left-hand path and continue along the lakeside. Climb a couple of stiles and turn left beside a wall. Follow the wall to another lake and walk beside the lake to a stile near a boathouse. Ignore a path on the right and continue alongside the lake but, just before the end of it, follow a left-hand fence away from the lake. Ignore a stile in the wall on the left and walk uphill to a lane. On your right, about 100 metres distant, is a standing stone.

Lane above Afon Mawddach

Turn left through a gate across the lane and follow the lane to a junction. Turn right and, after going through another gate, go left on a track signed unsuitable for motors. This is Ffordd Ddu (Black Road), an old road. Pass through a gate across it and notice to your right a conspicuous standing stone. Go through another gate and follow the track as it veers right. At the point where the track bends sharp left, leave it to go through a gate in the right-hand corner.

Walk downhill along a track with views of **Afon Mawddach** ahead of you. Emerge through a gate and cross directly over a lane to another. Continue walking ahead in the direction of Afon Mawddach. Pass a farm building on the right and a drive to a house. After about another 80 metres, take a track on the right. Go through a gate across the track and cross an old stone bridge over Afon Arthog. The flat area about 30 metres to your right was the site of **Llys Bradwen.**

Walk ahead to join a track and turn left to have great views of Afon Mawddach estuary. Pass through a gate and ignore a

Pared y Cefn Hir and Llynnau Cregennen

track on the left. Follow the track into a field and continue beside a wall on the left. Pass a barn on the left and turn left on a track. After a few paces, go through a gap on the right and veer slightly left across the field to a ladder stile. Continue ahead on a clear path to crags, then keep to the left above the crags and ignore another path that veers right.

Walk in the direction of a gate, with a house in the distance. Go through the gate and pass above a ruin. Climb a stile on the left and head slightly right downhill. Pass through a small gap, then bear left through another gap and follow the right-hand wall downhill to a lane. Turn right along it, uphill, to the start of the walk at the car park.

OTHER POINTS OF INTEREST

Afon Mawddach. This beautiful river starts its journey high on the boggy moors west of Llyn Tegid *(Bala Lake)* and plunges as a fall in Coed y Brenin Forest. Several other rivers join Afon Mawddach before it reaches the sea near Abermaw *(Barmouth)*.

The second lake

For several centuries, there were boatyards along many of the river's inlets, making oak sloops from the local woodlands. This ceased when the railways were built in the 19th century. On the north side of Afon Mawddach, the wild Rhinogydd mountains expose the oldest rocks in Snowdonia.

Standing Stone

Llys Bradwen. The only remains of this early medieval court are stone banks, partly covered with heather and grass. The lower enclosure is about 30 metres square and a slightly smaller one can be seen above it. Llys Bradwen *(Bradwen's Court)* was probably the court of a local chieftain, and it is said that a court was held here in the early 12th century.

29

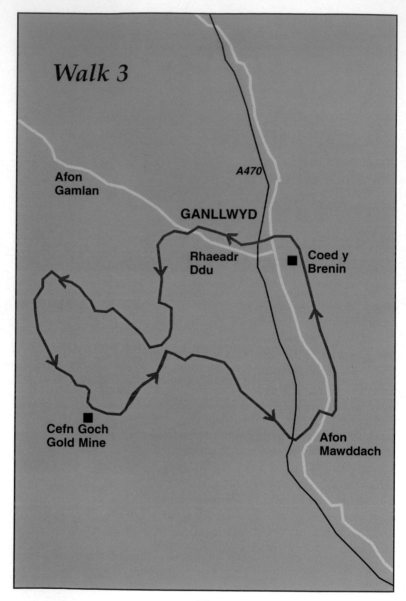

Walk 3

Afon
Gamlan

A470

GANLLWYD

Rhaeadr
Ddu

Coed y
Brenin

Cefn Goch
Gold Mine

Afon
Mawddach

3. Rhaeadr Ddu

Confluence Afon Gamlan with Afon Mawddach

Rhaeadr Ddu is a spectacular waterfall in Coed Ganllwyd, a nature reserve known for its mosses, liverworts and ferns. The ancient woodland consists mainly of sessile oak with some ash, birch and alder buckthorn. Birds to look out for include jay, nuthatch and pied flycatcher.

The walk – *after visiting viewpoints of the waterfalls, the route climbs gradually through woodlands and forest to pasture offering extensive views of the surrounding countryside. The site of a former gold mine is passed during the descent.*
5 miles – allow 3-4 hours.

Start at the car park in Ganllwyd village on the A470 north of Dolgellau. There is a bus stop nearby.

From the car park, walk out to the road. Cross and turn left then, in a few paces, bear right on a lane with a sign for Rhaeadr Ddu. With Afon Gamlan on your left, walk uphill and pass a drive to a farm on your right. After about 150 metres, at a right bend in the lane, take a path on the left waymarked with a green arrow.

Ignore a path on the left to a footbridge, but walk ahead to a viewpoint of Rhaeadr Ddu. Notice the **inscribed stone**. Go back a few paces along the path then descend to cross the footbridge spanning Afon Gamlan. Bear right along a rough path that climbs above the waterfalls. A short distance above the falls, bear left through trees on a waymarked path to a wall. Turn left, to have the wall on your right, and follow the path through the woodlands. Ignore a ladder stile on the right and take the waymarked path on the left.

Cross a small footbridge and go through a kissing-gate in a fence. On reaching a path junction, turn right and, after about 30 metres, go left through a small gate and cross a footbridge. After a few paces, bear right, with the stream on your right, to emerge on an access lane. Turn right and go through a gate into the forest. Ignore a track on the left and a footpath on the right. Stay on this main track and, on reaching a junction, where there is a gate on your right, leave the track to go ahead on a path with a post marked with white arrows.

The path winds uphill through the forest and, in places, is stony and wet. Higher up it joins a path marked with yellow arrows. On reaching a wall and gate, go through the gate and follow an old track. You have now left the forest. Join another track near a house and bear left to have great views over the surrounding countryside. At the end of sheep pens on the left, leave the track to walk below it, and pass just below an old barn. From this point the track can be seen re-entering the forest. Rejoin the track near a gate and cattle grid.

Go through the gate into the forest, much of which has been felled, opening up views. Just beyond a clearing, ignore a path on the right with a yellow arrow. Continue along the track for about 40 metres to a junction near a wall. Turn right and, after about 30 metres, climb a stile and cross a footbridge on the left. Slant to the right and follow a path over wet ground, then join a track and bear left. Remains of **Cefn-coch gold mine** crushing mill can be seen on your right.

Pass the remains of the mine barracks on your left. After a few more metres, climb a high ladder stile in a wall on your left, and walk downhill, following green arrows to another high stile in a right-hand corner. Continue ahead and, after passing a barn on your right, climb a stile near a gate to emerge on an access lane.

Turn right, downhill, and follow the lane until it emerges through a gate close to the A470. Turn right, passing houses, and cross the road to a footpath signpost. Follow the path downhill and soon Afon Mawddach is on your right. Emerge on a lane and cross a bridge over the river to **Coed y Brenin** Ty'n y Groes Forestry car park and picnic area.

Turn left to pass the car park and walk uphill along a track. Have the river on your left, and ignore a track on the right and paths leading off. Pass a track to a house on the left and, after about another 50 metres, go left to a kissing-gate. Follow the enclosed path to a footbridge over Afon Mawddach, and bear left uphill on a path to the car park at the start of the walk.

OTHER POINTS OF INTEREST
The Inscribed Stone. The tablet bears lines from a poem by Thomas Gray, but the original inscription is on another stone nearby. Poets visited William Alexander Madocks (1773-1828) when he lived at Dolmelynllyn, and they enjoyed the views of the waterfalls on the estate. Madocks created Porthmadog, the Cob embankment, a quay and Tremadog.

Cefn-coch gold mine. This mine was the third richest of the Meirionnydd gold mines. Gold was first discovered in this part of Wales during the 1840s, when mines near Gwynfynydd in Coed y Brenin were being worked for lead. The gold belt

Rhaeadr Ddu

Ruins of Cefn-coch gold mine

stretched from near Trawsfynydd to Bontddu, then west almost as far as Abermaw (Barmouth). The Cefn-coch mine was operated intermittently by different companies between 1862 and 1914. By the time the mine finally closed, nearly 1,400 oz of gold had been extracted.

Coed y Brenin Forest. This extensive forest was once part of the historic Nannau estate, which was founded about AD1100 by Cadwgan, son of the Prince of Powys. The estate stayed in the same family until the 18th century, when it passed through marriage to the Vaughan family. After the First World War, land was purchased from the estate to create the forest. The original name, Vaughan Forest, was changed to Coed y Brenin *(Forest of the King)* in 1935 to commemorate the Jubilee of King George V and Queen Mary. A herd of fallow deer from the former Nannau estate live on open land in Coed y Brenin.

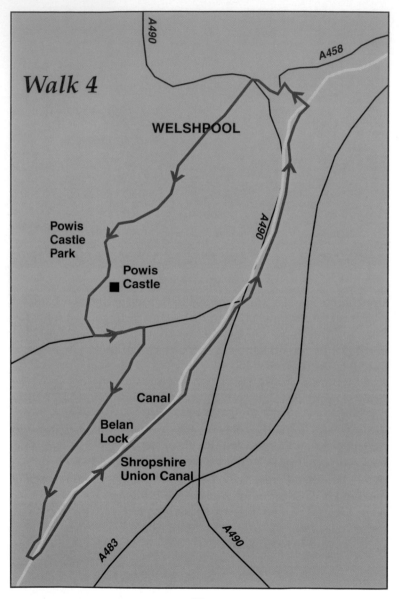

Walk 4

WELSHPOOL

A490

A458

Powis
Castle
Park

Powis
Castle

A490

Canal

Belan
Lock

Shropshire
Union Canal

A483

A490

4. Powis Castle
Tel: 01938 551929

Powis Castle and statue

The first castle here was a fortress built in the 13th century by Gruffudd ap Gwenwynwyn and his son Owain. Owain took the Norman name de la Pole and his daughter Hawys de la Pole married a Norman knight, John de Cherleton. Sir Edward Herbert acquired the castle in 1587 and he made many alterations. The Herbert family garrisoned the castle for the Royalists during the Civil War, but Parliamentary forces captured it in 1644. Heiress Lady Henrietta Herbert married Edward, the son of Clive of India, in 1784 and many of Clive's possessions were brought to the castle. There is a magnificent collection of paintings, tapestries and furniture as well as the Clive Museum. The magnificent gardens are known for their terraces, clipped yews and lead statues. Powis Castle was bequeathed to the National Trust in 1952.

Grace Evans's cottage

The walk – *after leaving Powis Castle Park, the walk climbs a small hill before descending through woods to the Montgomery Canal. The route then follows the towpath into Welshpool before returning to the start through the Lower Park.*
6 miles – about 3 hours

Start the walk at Powis Castle car park, which is accessed from a lane off the A490 south of Welshpool. Buses and trains travel to Welshpool. The route passes through the town.

From the car park, walk towards the castle, and instead of taking the drive to the castle, go ahead along the drive signed Way Out. At the end of the drive, there is a kissing-gate a few paces to the right of the cattle grid.

Turn left along the lane and pass a drive to Dyserth Hall on your right. When the entrance drive to Powis Castle is on your left, bear right over a stile next to a field gate. Go ahead and follow a track, passing trees on your right. After the track bends left over a bridge, go through a gate and immediately turn right to cross a stile.

Walk ahead and soon veer left to walk uphill beside a right-hand fence. To your left are extensive views over the Severn Valley. In the top right-hand corner of the field, climb a stile and continue along the right boundary to a kissing-gate. Walk ahead, veering slightly left up the hill, and you will soon have a fence and trees on your left. Pass a waymark and continue above the wood until you reach a wider path at a fence above the woods.

At a corner, climb a stile into the wood and follow the path as it gradually goes downhill to a stile near a gate. Cross a stream and pass the garden of a bungalow, then go through a kissing-gate to a lane. Turn left to cross a bridge over the **Montgomery Canal** and, after a few paces, go right through a gate onto the canal towpath.

Turn right along the towpath and follow it to Belan Lock. Go below the road bridge and pass the lock and a picnic area. Continue beside the canal, which eventually bends right under a road. Cross a causeway at a nature reserve and bear left. After emerging on a lane, continue beside the canal. Powisland Museum can be seen on the opposite side of the canal. Go under a road bridge and, a little further on, cross a footbridge over the canal.

After passing a car park, you will arrive at a road junction in the centre of Welshpool. The route goes left here, but to your right is **St Mary' Parish Church** and, further on, below the church, is **Grace Evan's Cottage.**

Continuing on the walk, you will reach a crossroads at traffic lights. Turn right along Broad Street and pass New Street with its **Cockpit** on your left. Pass the Town Hall on your right and, in another 50 metres, turn left at a signpost for Powis Castle.

Go through the gate into the Lower Park. There is a pond in trees below on the left. Pass through another gate and continue along the drive. Ignore the left-hand fork and walk ahead to the start of your walk at the car park.

Montgomery Canal Milepost

Powis Castle Park

OTHER POINTS OF INTEREST

The Montgomery Canal. A scheme of waterways was planned in the late 18th century to link the Severn, Mersey and Dee rivers. The Montgomershire Canal Act was duly authorised and the section from Welsh Frankton to Llanymynech opened in 1796. A year later the canal passed through Welshpool, but it did not reach Newtown until 1821. The many goods transported along the Montgomery Canal included limestone, coal, timber, dairy produce and grain, and the canal at Welshpool was lined with warehouses. Road and rail took over, but the waterway was in use until 1936 when it was breached near Welsh Frankton. The canal is now known for its wildlife, and much of it is a Site of Scientific Interest. Its aquatic vegetation is the habitat of many dragonflies and damselflies. As you walk along the towpath, you will be following a section of the long distance footpath, The Severn Way.

Welshpool. This borderlands market town was granted a charter in 1263 by Gwenwynwyn, Prince of Powys. Many historic buildings line the broad streets, and some of them are half-timbered , dating back to the 16th century.

St Mary's Church. The parish church dates from the mid 13th century, but only the lower part of the tower remains from the original church. Inside are several monuments to the Earls of Powis. There is a memorial to Bishop William Morgan who was vicar of the church 1575-1579. He translated the Bible into Welsh in 1588, and his birthplace, Tŷ Mawr Wybrnant, near Penmachno, northern Wales, is a National Trust property. Outside St Mary's Church, opposite the church door, is a stone said to be part of the abbot's throne at Strata Marcella Abbey.

Grace Evans' Cottage. Grace Evans was a maid to the Countess of Nithsdale, who was a daughter of the Earl of Powis. The Earl of Nithsdale was condemned to death and imprisoned in the Tower of London after taking part in the 1715 Jacobite Rebellion. With the help of Grace Evans, the Countess dressed her husband in women's clothes and smuggled him out of the

Belan Lock

The Cockpit

tower. To thank her, the Nithsdales gave Grace Evans this cottage.

The Cockpit. The only cockpit in Wales still standing on its original site is this one in Welshpool. It was in use from the early 18th century until 1849, when cockfighting was made illegal.

Powis Castle

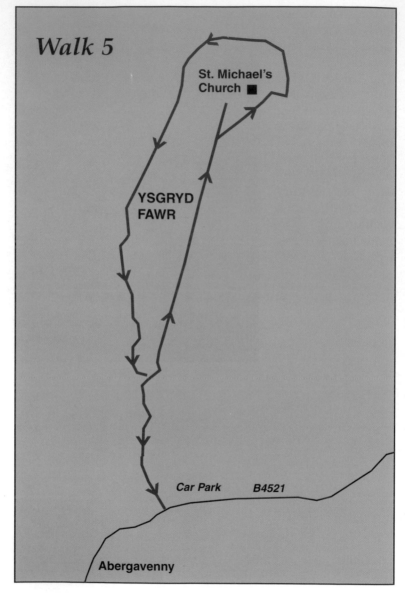

Walk 5

St. Michael's
Church ■

YSGRYD
FAWR

Car Park   B4521

Abergavenny

44

5. Ysgryd Fawr

Ysgryd Fawr

With an elevation of 486 metres, Ysgryd Fawr is an isolated, red sandstone hill in the Black Mountains. On the western slopes is an odd looking landslip, and the mountain's strange shape has given rise to a number of legends. According to one story, the mountain was torn in two at the time of Christ's crucifixion. The remains of St Michael's medieval chapel are still visible on the summit.

The walk – *a steady climb through woodlands and along the ridge to the summit of Ysgryd Fawr. After descending the eastern flank, the route traverses around the mountain to return along the western side.* 4 miles – allow 2-3 hours

Remains of St. Michael's Chapel

Ysgryd Fawr

Start at a lay-by, south of Ysgryd Fawr and on the B4521, about two miles east of Abergavenny. Abergavenny is a stop on the Cardiff-Manchester railway line.

From the car park, take the stony track at the sign for Ysgryd Fawr. Ignore a stile into a field and bear right with the track in the direction of a wood. Cross a stile at the edge of the wood and follow the main path for about 30 metres before going right on a path that soon goes up steps.

Walk uphill through the trees and cross over a track to continue climbing. Go through a small gate and turn right beside a wall. After about 40 metres, leave the wall to go left and up more steps. The path becomes stony and then veers slightly right to climb up out of the trees.

Take the path up to the ridge of Ysgryd Fawr and enjoy views of **Abergavenny** and the surrounding countryside. To the west is cone shaped Y Fal (Sugar Loaf) and south-west is the massive hill Blorens (Blorenge). Follow the ridge to the summit where you will find the remains of **St Michael's Chapel** and a trig. point.

Walk back the way you came for about 100 metres and pass a small hollow on your left. After about another 50 metres, take a path on the left. It soon turns sharp left to go downhill through bracken.

On reaching a footpath signpost, bear right. The path drops down to a crossroads of paths where you turn left. Pass a post with a yellow arrow and, about 50 metres before reaching a fence, turn left. After a few paces, you will reach a corner fence. Here, the path becomes clearer as it passes through bracken and crosses a stream.

Pass the landslip and descend into trees. After following the path for about a mile you will have a wall on your right. Continue beside it until you reach a small gate. This is the gate you came through earlier on the walk before climbing to the ridge of Ysgryd Fawr. Go through the gate and walk downhill to retrace your steps to the start of the walk.

Abergavenny Castle

OTHER POINTS OF INTEREST

Abergavenny. This attractive market town lies at the confluence of Afon Gafenni with Afon Wysg *(River Usk)*. The strategic importance of the site was recognised by the Romans and they had a fort here called Gobannium. The Normans built a castle on the hill above Afon Wysg, and it is remembered for the treachery of William de Braose. In 1175 he invited the local chieftain Seisyllt ap Dyfnwal and chiefs to a banquet on Christmas Day. During the feast, de Braose and his men slaughtered them. A few years later, Hywel ab Iorwerth of Caerleon burnt the castle. Several unsuccessful attempts, were made by the Welsh to kill de Braose, but he finally met his fate when King John took away his land so that he died a beggar. St Mary's Church in Abergavenny is the burial place of several Marcher lords.

St. Mary's Church

St Michael's Chapel. The chapel was a simple, rectangular building and its outline is recognizable from the low banks south of the trig. point. Only two upright stones remain standing. Little is known of the medieval chapel's history, but it stood at the meeting point of three parishes. It is said that, in the 17th century, when Catholics were being persecuted, more than one hundred worshippers would climb the hill to attend Mass. The mountain was thought to be holy, and local people collected soil from the lower slopes and scattered it in their fields to improve the crops.

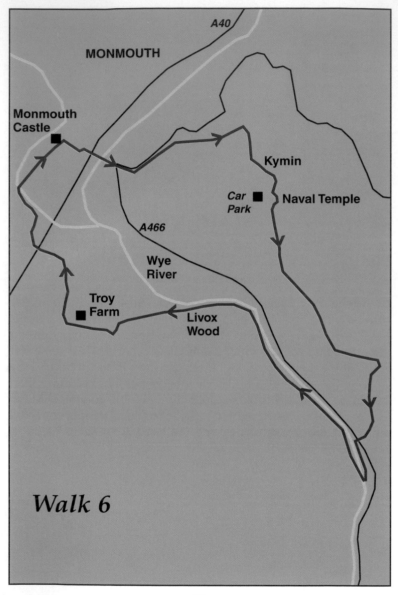

Walk 6

6. The Kymin
Tel: 01600 719241

The Kymin, the Round House

From The Kymin are spectacular views stretching as far as the mountains beyond Abergavenny. On top of the 840 foot hill are two interesting Georgian buildings. The banqueting house is a small, circular two-storied tower built in 1794 as a dining club. Nearby, the naval temple was erected in 1800 to celebrate the victories of the British Navy. Above it is Britannia seated on a rock. Nelson visited the site in July 1802 after sailing up the River Wye to Monmouth. He and his companions ate their breakfast in the Round House. The National Trust acquired the property in 1902.

Agincourt Square

The walk – *descends the Offa's Dyke Path to the River Wye and crosses the footbridge over the river to take a bridleway along the riverbank. After visiting Monmouth, the route rejoins the Offa's Dyke Path and follows it back to the start.*
8 miles – allow 4-5 hours

Start at The Kymin car park, reached by a lane off the A4136, near Monmouth. Those using public transport should start in Monmouth. Buses run from Hereford, Abergavenny and Chepstow to Monmouth.

From the car park, cross the lane to a kissing-gate. Follow the path to another kissing-gate and continue downhill along the right side of the field to a stile and an enclosed path. Emerge in a field and cross it to another stile, then walk ahead towards a building on the right.

Before reaching the corner of the field, climb a stile on your right. Join a track coming from the house and walk downhill. Pass a farm on the left and continue downhill. Ignore a track on the left and, further downhill, emerge onto a road.

Turn right and ignore an Offa's Dyke Path sign on the left. Go under a bridge and follow the pavement to the A466. Bear right for a few metres then cross the road to a footpath (The Wye Valley Walk). With the river nearby on your right, follow the slightly overgrown path until it goes up steps to benches. Turn right on a level path and, in a few paces, go right on a path to cross a footbridge over the River Wye beside an old railway bridge.

On reaching the other side of the river, turn right to pass The Boat Inn and, a few metres further on, bear right through a gate to have the River Wye on your right. Go through a small gate and walk through a field, passing below a house to another gate. Continue ahead to Washing Wood, and ignore a path on the left that goes uphill. Continue beside the river and follow the path out of the trees and through bracken to a small gate.

Walk through a big field and continue through gates. Have

Monnow Bridge

River Wye

trees to your left and, at the end of the field, climb a stile into Livox Wood. A clear path goes through the trees to a stile at the other end of the wood.

Go ahead through the field, away from the river, and gently uphill to a track that enters trees, then bears right to have a field on the left. Pass through double gates to reach several tracks. Keep directly ahead to farm buildings at Troy Farm, then bear right to have the farmhouse some distance to your right.

The Naval Temple

Follow the wide track and cross a bridge over Afon Troddi *(River Trothy)*.

Emerge onto a road and turn right along the pavement, ignoring a road on the right. The road you are on passes above the A40 and goes downhill to a junction. Turn left and ignore the first bridge on your right that crosses the River Monnow. Continue to a small roundabout in Over Monnow. St Thomas's Church is on your right.

Bear right and cross **Monnow Bridge** into Monmouth. Walk ahead along the street to **Agincourt Square.** Castle Hill Road on the left leads to the ruins of **Monmouth Castle.** If you continue along the main street as it curves to the left you will see the **Nelson Museum.**

Return to the Shire Hall and go along pedestrianised Church Street to St Mary's Street and turn right to a junction.

Bear left along St James's Street and, in a few paces, turn right along a road. Use the subway on your left to go under the A40. On leaving the subway, bear right, then left to cross the bridge over the River Wye.

When the road bends right, continue ahead on the A4136. Pass the Mayhill Hotel on your right and follow the road as it curves left uphill. At the end of the right-hand pavement, take a railed path that runs above the road. Emerge onto a track and walk ahead to a lane, then continue uphill.

Leave the lane where it bends right by taking a kissing-gate into woodland. Go ahead through the trees on the main path. Higher up, the path curves to the right and, when it bends left, go through a kissing-gate on your right. Walk uphill to another kissing-gate and turn left, uphill, along a lane.

Ignore a stile on the left and, after a few more paces, go through a kissing-gate on the left into woodland. Walk ahead uphill and when a fence on the right ends bear right over a banking then immediately turn left on a path. It rises to a stepped path with a National Trust plaque. Emerge at a footpath signpost and bear right, passing The Kymin and The Temple, to the car park.

OTHER PLACES OF INTEREST

Monnow Bridge. This is the only fortified bridge built in the medieval period in Britain that is still standing. The bridge itself was built in 1272, and the gatehouse was added about 25 years later as part of the town's defences. It also served as a tollgate. Originally, the bridge was narrower than it is now. It was widened in the early 19th century, when the passageways were constructed. Nowadays, it is only used by pedestrians.

Agincourt Square. The Shire Hall was built in 1724 on the site of a former Elizabethan market hall. A statue of Henry V is in a niche on the front of the building, and there is a statue of Charles Rolls, a co-founder of the Rolls-Royce company, in the square. The Rolls family had an estate outside Monmouth.

Charles Rolls began by importing and selling French built cars. He met Henry Royce and in 1906 they created the Silver Ghost. He was also interested in aeroplanes and, in June 1910, was the first person to fly both ways across the English Channel in a single journey. On the 12th of July of the same year, he died in a flying competition at Bournemouth. He was the first person to die in a flying accident.

Monmouth Castle. Only fragments remain of the once important Norman Castle founded in the 11th century by William FitzOsbern to guard the Wye and Monnow rivers. All that can be seen today is the ruined Great Tower and Hall. Henry V was born in the Great Tower in 1387. The single-storey Hall was built in the mid 13th century by the Earl of Lancaster, and it was used for the holding of courts until the 17th century. There was a gatehouse on Castle Hill Road, and a large keep stood on the site of the present Great Castle House. The Norman castle was destroyed in 1647 during the Civil War, and The Marquis of Worcester built the Great Castle House in 1673, which is now the Headquarters of the Royal Monmouthshire Royal Engineers. The Regimental Museum is housed in a 19th century wing.

Nelson Museum. Lady Llangattock, the mother of Charles Rolls, collected artefacts and memorabilia relating to Nelson and she bequeathed the collection to the town in 1924. The collection is in the museum and there are also displays about the history of the area.

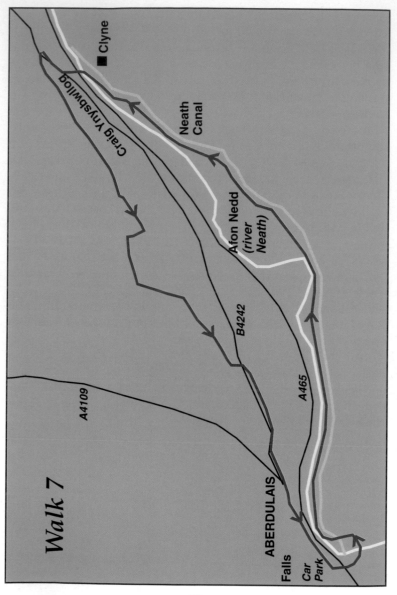

Walk 7

Clyne

Craig Ynysbwllog

Neath Canal

Afon Nedd
(river Neath)

B4242

A465

A4109

ABERDULAIS

Falls

Car Park

58

7. Aberdulais Falls

Tel: 01639 636674

Aberdulais Falls

The industrial heritage of this beautiful waterfall goes back to 1584 when a copper smelting furnace was established beside Afon Dulais. By the middle of the 18th century, there was a large flour mill on the site and, in the 1790s, the artist Turner visited and painted Aberdulais Falls. The industrial ruins on the site today are the remains of tin-plate works that opened in 1830 and operated for 60 years.

Since acquiring the site in 1981, the National Trust have embarked on a hydro-electric project to harness the waters of Afon Dulais. The huge waterwheel drives an alternator that produces ample electricity for the property. There is also a turbine generating electricity for the National Grid. A fish pass has been installed to enable salmon and sea trout to swim to the upper reaches of Afon Dulais.

Aberdulais Aqueduct

The walk – *takes the towpath beside the Neath Canal to Clyne, the route then climbs through woodlands to a Roman Road and follows it back to the valley.*

6 miles – 3 hours

Start at the car park for Aberdulais Falls (or from the nearby lay-by) on the A4109, north-west of Neath. Buses run from Swansea, Neath and other towns to Aberdulais Falls.

From the car park, cross the road at the traffic lights and take a path beside the river and under a road. Reach a road from where you can see **Aberdulais Aqueduct.** Go ahead to walk under a bridge and emerge on a road. Turn left over a bridge and pass The Railway Tavern.

After a few metres, turn left at a sign for the **Aberdulais Canal Basin.** Walk under a bridge then bear right to cross the old skew bridge. Turn right and have the Neath Canal on your right. Go around a barrier and walk ahead. Pass bridges and locks, and ignore a footbridge over the canal. On your left is the

Lock on Neath Canal

River Neath.

After going through a kissing-gate, cross a footbridge over the River Neath. Take a path under the road bridge and turn right along a pavement. After about 100 metres, turn left on a path and follow it up the wooded, steep hill. A stream tumbles down on your right. The path soon curves to the left and levels out. Maintain your direction as it gradually starts to climb and become a track.

Cross a stile beside a gate and, at a fork, take the right-hand track. There are soon good views across the valley. Follow the track as it bears right and shortly turns left. On reaching a crossroads of tracks, with signs left and right for Byway Cilffordd, turn left through a gate and follow the track, **Sarn Helen,** downhill.

Go left at a fork and continue downhill. The track curves to the right and has a field on the right. It goes through gates and is very stony as it descends between walls. The track bends left and passes a Sarn Helen sign.

Emerge on a road and cross to a pavement, then turn right.

River Neath

You will pass works, a road on the right and woodlands. Follow the pavement until you reach the start of the walk near Aberdulais Falls.

OTHER POINTS OF INTEREST

Aberdulais Aqueduct. Just beyond the confluence of Afon Dulais and the River Neath (Afon Nedd), and a weir, the Aberdulais Aqueduct spans the river. It is 340 foot long with ten arches. The aqueduct was built in 1823 to link the Tennant Canal with the Aberdulais Basin and the Neath Canal. Opened in 1824, the eight mile Tennant Canal ends at Port Tennant, Swansea. Look for a plaque about Alexander Cordell's novel 'Song of the Earth'. Nearby was the lock keeper's cottage.

Aberdulais Canal Basin. The Neath and Tennant Canals never operated as one company, although they interconnected at the Aberdulais Basin. At a meeting between Lord Vernon and local people in 1790, it was decided that a canal from Pontneddfechan (Glyn Neath) to Neath would benefit the area. An Act of

Weir, River Neath

Parliament was passed a year later. Completed in 1795, it was extended to Giant's Grave near Britton Ferry in 1799. The full length of the canal is 13 miles. Navigation on the canal ceased in 1934. Some of the locks have been restored, and a four mile section from Glyn Neath to Resolven is navigable.

Sarn Helen. The Romans met a lot of opposition from the tribe called the Silures when they tried to conquer this part of Wales. It took the Romans from AD49 to AD77 to overpower them. The Romans built legionary and auxiliary forts, marching camps and roads. This military road linked the fort near Brecon with the auxiliary fort of Nidum at Neath. The name Sarn Helen is thought to be derived from the legendary Welsh wife of Magnus Maximus.

Sarn Helen

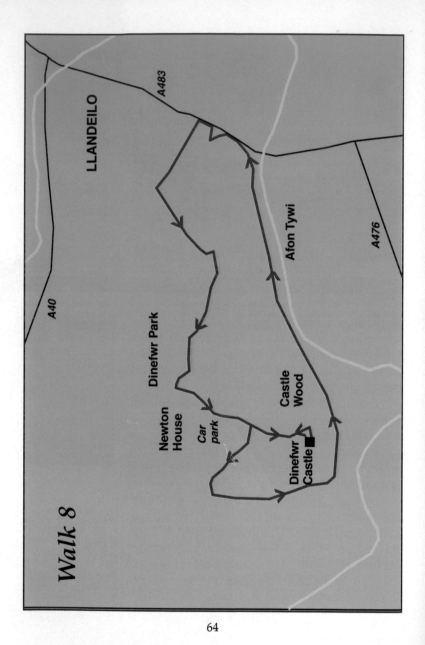

Walk 8

LLANDEILO

A483

A40

A476

Afon Tywi

Dinefwr Park

Newton House

Car park

Castle Wood

Dinefwr Castle

8. Dinefwr Park

Tel: 01558 823902

Dinefwr Castle

Dinefwr Park lies on hilly ground on the north side of the Tywi valley. Newton House, the main focus, was built in the mid 17th century by the Rhys (Rice) family on the site of a former 13th century English settlement. Since then, the mansion has been altered and now has a mid 19th century Gothic façade. There are some small, interesting buildings in the grounds, including an ice house. It is thought the landscape of the park was influenced by Capability Brown, who visited Dinefwr in the late 18th century. There is a herd of fallow deer, and the white park cattle have been bred at Dinefwr for about one thousand years. Newton House and most of the estate are now owned by the National Trust, whilst part is managed by the Wildlife Trust (SW Wales) and Cadw.

Dinefwr Castle

The walk – *visits the ruins of Dinefwr Castle, then heads towards the river meadows and the town of Llandeilo, returning to the start via Llandyfeisant Church.*
5 miles – 3 hours

Start the walk at Dinefwr Park Visitor Centre on the outskirts of Llandeilo. There are buses to Llandeilo from Carmarthen. Llandeilo is on the Heart of Wales Railway Line, which runs between Shrewsbury and Swansea.

At the car park, have your back to the Visitor Centre and turn right to a track. Bear right to go through a small gate next to a cattle grid and follow the track to a fork. Bear right beside a wall and continue along the track, then through a gate across it. Pass a building and go through two kissing-gates next to gates across the track.

After a few paces, leave the track to go uphill to a kissing-gate and enter Castle Wood. Follow the path to a track and turn right to the ruins of **Dinefwr Castle.**

Retrace your steps through the woods and down the hill to the lower track. Turn left and go through another kissing-gate into a wood. Pass the Mill Pond and the Pump House on your right, and continue on the track through mature woodland. The track goes downhill, with views of pools below on your right, to a stile and field.

Head across the field to a kissing-gate about 100 metres right of the left-hand corner of the field. Above on your left is Dinefwr Castle ruins. Go slightly left and through a gate into the next field, then straight ahead. Ignore a stile on the right to the riverbank.

At sheep pens, cross a flat bridge and go through a kissing-gate next to a field gate. Follow the track to a kissing-gate just beyond a broad gate near a wood and house. Turn right to Llandeilo Bridge spanning Afon Tywi.

Turn left along the pavement up Bridge Street into **Llandeilo**. Before reaching the church, go left towards The

Afon Tywi

Dinefwr Park

King's Head and bear right up a steep hill. At the Old Bank (a branch of the Black Ox) on your left, go through a kissing-gate into the churchyard. On your left, under the beech trees, is the interesting grave of carpenter and diarist Thomas Jenkins. Continue through the churchyard to the road. On the opposite side is the entrance gate to **St Teilo's Church.**

Follow the road uphill and pass a small park. Ignore King Street on the left, but take the next road left,

Carmarthen Street. You will pass on your right the Old Shire Hall and, higher up, on your left the former school. To your right is the Provision Market, and on your left a track leads into **Parc Penlan**.

Continue along the road and turn left along Dinefwr Park drive. On reaching trees on your left, go left through a small gate into the woodland. The path runs parallel to the road for about 100 metres, then descends to a track at a wall. Turn left on the track and, after a few paces, go right down steps to Llandyfeisant Church, closed since 1961.

Walk past the church and, on the other side, go through a small gate and down steps into Dinefwr Park. Walk ahead up the hill to a stile at a gate. Maintain your direction and pass trees on your right. After a few more metres, veer right to gates and the park drive. Turn left along the drive to the start of the walk at the car park.

OTHER POINTS OF INTEREST
Dinefwr Castle. Traditionally (although it is not proven) the site of the castle dates back to the 9th century when Rhodri Fawr is reputed to have had a stronghold here. He divided Wales into three kingdoms – Gwynedd (northern), Powys (central) and Deheubarth (southern). The powerful Lord Rhys (Rhys ap Gruffudd), ruler of Deheubarth, erected a fortification on the site c.1163, and it was probably a stone castle. His son Rhys Gryg may have built the keep. A small Welsh settlement became established on flat ground nearby. Edward 1 captured the castle and made alterations. In 1298, he founded a new English settlement near the site of the present Newton House. The two towns prospered and were granted a charter in 1363. Dinefwr Castle withstood Owain Glyndŵr's rebellion in 1403, but afterwards the towns went into decline. A new mansion was built by the Rhys (Rice) family at Newton in the 16th century, although by then little remained of the town. Dinefwr Castle was deliberately altered in the 18th century into a romantic ruin,

Dinefwr Park Cattle

designed to give pleasure to those who visited the estate.

Llandeilo. The town takes its name from St Teilo who founded a religious community here in the 6th century. By the 9th century, it was the centre of the Bishop of St Teilo, and was known as Llandeilo Fawr, the Great Llan of St Teilo. During the 12th century, control passed to Talley Abbey, and it later became a possession of St David's. The town developed commercially during the medieval period and a grant was issued in 1291 to hold a fair. By the 1400s it was a bigger township than Dinefwr. The streets around the churchyard were the heart of Llandeilo, and a well in the churchyard, near the church, supplied the townsfolk with their water. (In the 19th century, it was covered over and its outlet is now through a conduit in Church Street.) The steep hill past The King's Head was the main route through the town until a road was cut through the churchyard in the early 19th century. A branch of the Black Ox Bank opened in 1842, and it issued its own bank notes. Llandeilo Bridge, spanning Afon Tywi, was completed in 1848. The town has many fine 18th and 19th century houses.

St Teilo's Church. Teilo is said to have been born at Penally, near Tenby, in the 6th century, and to have been educated by St David. According to legend, he accompanied St David and St Padarn to Rome and the Holy Land. After returning to Wales, he founded the monastery at Llandeilo and travelled through south-east Wales, converting people and building churches. A dispute arose between the churches of Penally, Llandeilo and Llandaff when he died, because each church claimed the right to have his relics. It is said that his body miraculously tripled itself so that each church had a body to bury.

The religious community grew at Llandeilo and it became one of the most important in Wales. About 820 AD it was given a fine gospel book by a man called Gelhi. Margins in the book were used to record local transactions and settlements. For an unknown reason, the

Newton House

book was given in the 11th century to Lichfield, and it is now kept in the cathedral, where it is called the Lichfield or St Chad Gospels. In Llandeilo the book is referred to as the Llandeilo Gospels. A digital copy is now the centrepiece of an exhibition in St Teilo's Church in Llandeilo.

In the foyer there is a 15th century font from Llandyfeisant Church. Two Celtic crosses, both dating from the 8th century, can be seen in a small side chapel. The church was rebuilt in the mid 19th century except for the tower, which is medieval.

Parc Penlan. The park is located above the town and high above the Tywi valley. It offers fine views of the surrounding countryside. Lord Dynevor gave the land as a gift to the town, and it was officially opened in June 1908. At the time, the town had two bands, so a bandstand was built with seats and shelters.

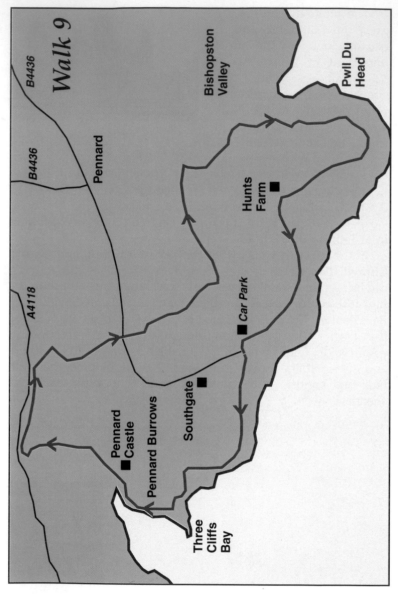

Walk 9

B4436

B4436

A4118

Pennard

Bishopston Valley

Pwll Du Head

Hunts Farm

Car Park

Southgate

Pennard Castle

Pennard Burrows

Three Cliffs Bay

9. PEППARD CLIFFS

Pennard Castle ruins

These spectacular, limestone cliffs stretch from Pwll Du Head in the east to Three Cliffs Bay in the West. This area of common land was acquired by the National Trust in 1954. On East Cliff there are caves that, on excavation, revealed bones of animals now extinct in Britain. Minchin Hole produced bones of bison, hyena, elephant and rhinoceros. Finds in the cave indicate it was occupied by man during the Iron Age and early Medieval period.

The walk – *follows the cliffs to Three Cliffs Bay, then goes through the dunes to Pennard Castle, returning through woods and fields. The longer walk visits Bishopston Valley and Pwll Du Head before returning to the start.*
5 or 8 miles – 3 or 5 hours

Start at the National Trust Pennard Cliffs car park at Southgate. Buses run from Swansea. There is a bus stop in the village near the car park.

From the car park, walk towards the sea and a footpath signpost. Turn right along an access lane and pass above **Heatherslade.** Just before reaching the end of the lane, go left on a path. Walk along the cliff tops until you see **Three Cliffs Bay** ahead. Keep above the cliffs and veer right to take a path that descends into a sandy valley (called Pobbles valley).

Join another path in the valley and turn left to Pobbles beach. After exploring it, return to the valley path and, after about 100 metres, go left on a partly stepped path. Go left along a board walk above the valley, which bears right to give good views of the cliffs.

On reaching a footpath signpost, ignore the path on the left to **Penmaen Burrows** and continue ahead. The path goes downhill through the dunes. Walk ahead, uphill, on a board walk and maintain your direction to the ruins of **Pennard Castle.**

Continue ahead on the path across the golf course and enter woodlands. Walk downhill through the trees to a path junction. Turn right and, at a footbridge on the left, go ahead up a stepped path to follow the path along the wooded hillside. On reaching footpath signs, ignore the right-hand path and go slightly left beside a fence.

Emerge on a lane and cross it to a track. Ignore a footbridge on the left and, immediately after passing houses, bear right on a narrow path beside a fence. The path widens and goes gently uphill through trees and, after becoming fenced, emerges on a road near houses. Turn right and ignore a road on the left. Walk uphill and, when the road bends to the right downhill, go left on a track. On reaching a fork, go left and emerge where two roads meet.

Cross the main road to a walking man signpost and, after going up steps, bear right through a kissing-gate. Pass through

Pennard Pill Estuary

another kissing-gate and follow an enclosed path to its end, then cross a stile on the left. Walk along the enclosed path to another stile and field. Walk along the left boundary of three fields. In the last field, cross the corner stile and bear right on a path through trees to a stile and field. Follow the right-hand fence to a stile on the right and go ahead to a track. (For the shorter walk, bear right for about 500 metres to the car park.)

For the longer walk, turn left along the track and, after passing a house on the left, follow a path to a gate. Walk along the rather muddy track to a path junction and turn left, then quickly right, to go downhill to a path junction beside the river in **Bishopston Valley.**

Turn right beside the river and go up a few steps to follow an uphill path. On reaching a fork, where the path on the left descends, take the right-hand path that goes directly ahead. Walk up to emerge in a field and turn left to where the field tapers into a corner. Climb a stile in the right-hand corner and

Two views of the Three Cliffs

walk ahead to a stile on the right side of a house. Follow a fence on the left to another stile and join a track.

Turn right on the track and enjoy the views on your left over **Pwll Du Bay**. When the track bears right, turn left to a footpath signpost. Go through a gate then climb a stile and follow a footpath through fields to a stile above the cliffs.

The path goes downhill to a path junction. Turn right to pass above a place called **Graves End** on the eastern slopes of **Pwll Du Head**. The cliff path climbs above **Deepslade** otherwise known as Hunts Bay to a lane near Hunts Farm. Bear left and, after passing the farm, follow a grassy path that runs between the cliffs and lane. It emerges near the start of the walk at the car park.

OTHER POINTS OF INTEREST

Heatherslade. This is the name of a small, rocky bay below Pennard Cliffs, just a few hundred metres west of the car park. The poet Vernon Watkins (1906-1967) lived for a time in a house here that had the same name. His titles include 'Battle of the Mari Lwyd' and 'Lady with the Unicorn'.

Three Cliffs Bay. The name is derived from the three pointed cliffs in the bay. It is the estuary of the Pennard Pill and there is an area of salt marsh to the east. Sea bathing is dangerous here.

Penmaen Burrows. This National Trust property is the headland on the opposite side of the bay. It was acquired in 1967 and has several archaeological sites, including the remains of a large Neolithic burial chamber and the earthworks of a Norman castle. There is also a large man-made rabbit warren. The remains of a tiny, medieval church were uncovered in the 19th century.

Pennard Castle. The first castle on the site was probably built by Henry de Beaumont who was granted the lordship of Gŵyr in the early 11th century. Little remains of this castle and the ruins still standing are of a masonry castle built in the 13th century. It is thought to be the work of the de Braose family, Norman rulers

Pwll Du Head

of Gŵyr. By 1321, it was in the hands of the de Mowbray family. The castle had a curtain wall around a courtyard and a twin towered gatehouse. A settlement grew around the castle, but encroaching sand in the following centuries caused the abandonment of the castle and village.

A local legend tells the story of the abandoned castle. It is said that, whilst enjoying his marriage feast, the chieftain of Pennard Castle became annoyed with fairies who were playing music. He tried to kill them but, as they were bloodless, they could not be killed by his stabbings. Eventually, he was told he would be punished because of his war against the elves. Whirlwinds of sand, said to be from Ireland, overwhelmed the castle and houses.

Bishopston Valley. Ancient woodland survives in this sheltered, secluded, limestone valley owned by the National Trust. The stream is partly subterranean but, in wet weather, flows mostly above ground. There is an Iron Age promontory fort on the east side of the valley. Limestone quarries were once worked here.

Pwll Du Bay. The name in English means Black Pool and it is derived from the pool behind the storm beach. There used to be two public houses and quarrymen's cottages at Pwll Du. The bay was a haunt of smugglers and the contraband was taken up the valley and hidden in farm cellars until it could be distributed safely.

Graves End. This spot marks the burial place of over sixty men who died in November 1760 when an Admiralty ship was wrecked on rocks off Pwll Du headland. In the vessel's hold were pressgang victims. The ship was bound for Plymouth , but it changed course because of bad weather and the crew thought Pwll Du Head was Mumbles Head. The crew were able to scramble ashore, but the men in the hold could not escape. Their bodies were washed ashore the next morning. They were buried in a common grave at the place called Graves End.

Pwll Du Head. To the west of the headland is a small Iron Age promontory fort with two lines of ramparts. It was occupied up to the second century AD, and excavations uncovered animal bones and pottery.

Deepslade (or Hunts Bay). In the cliffs west of the bay is the excavated bone cave known as Bacon Hole. The name originates from the red oxide stripes on the cave wall – they were thought to resemble streaky bacon.

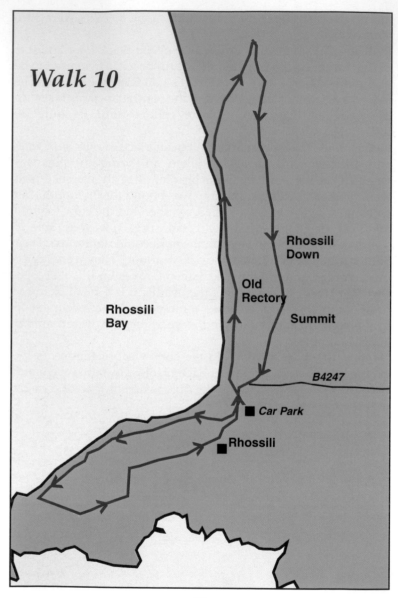

Walk 10

Rhossili
Down

Old
Rectory

Summit

Rhossili
Bay

B4247

■ *Car Park*

■ Rhossili

10. Rhossili Visitor Centre
Tel: 01792 390707

Burry Holms in Rhossili Bay

The Visitor Centre is in a former coastguard cottage on the cliffs above Rhossili beach. It is an interpretation centre for Gŵyr. The National Trust owns many properties on the peninsula, and those around Rhossili were acquired in 1967.

The Walk – *goes along the cliffs to a spectacular viewpoint of Worms Head, then inland to St Mary's Church. From the church, scenic paths are followed below Rhossili Down and along the hilltop.*
6 miles – 3-4 hours

Start the walk at the car park in Rhossili village, near the western tip of Gŵyr (Gower). Buses run to Rhossili from Swansea.

From the car park, bear left and pass the Visitor Centre. From

Rhossili Church

here are great views over **Rhossili Bay**. Go through the gate and follow the track heading towards **Worms Head.** At a corner of the left-hand wall, continue ahead to the old Coastguard Lookout to have clear views of the tidal island.

From the lookout, walk away from the cliffs and take a path slanting towards a wall. Reach the wall at a corner and follow a path around the corner to a kissing-gate in another stretch of wall. Go through the kissing-gate and continue along the track to a junction and turn left. After about 200 metres, the track bears right. When another track joins it, bear left to the road.

Take a path passing **St Mary's Church** but ignore the path to Rhossili Beach, and go through a gate onto Rhossili Down. Ignore a path on the right and follow a path beside the left-hand wall and along the lower slopes of **Rhossili Down**. You will soon have good views of the beach and the island of **Burry Holms** at the northern end of the bay. Cross a footbridge and follow the path behind the **Old Rectory.** Further on, you will pass a caravan site that is behind a wall on the left. When there is a gate on the left at the entrance to the caravan park, bear right uphill on a path.

Cross over a path and, further on, at rocks where the track goes downhill, go left on a narrower path. Below on your left are the Sweyn Howes Neolithic burial chambers. Below on the right are the remains of a radar station.

Join the broader track and follow it to the trig. point. Go ahead, downhill, on the broad path and ignore another path on the left. On reaching a wall corner on your left, take a path on the right. The path is partly stepped lower down the hill.

Join the outward route at the gate giving access to Rhossili Down. Walk ahead towards the church, and take a path to pass the church on your left, then go right to the car park and Visitor Centre.

OTHER POINTS OF INTEREST

Rhossili Bay. This unspoiled beach is three miles long and is popular with surfers. Several ships have been wrecked in the bay and the wooden ribs of the *Helvetia*, stranded in 1887, are exposed at low tide. All the crew escaped and the cargo of timber was recovered, but five men drowned when one of the salvage boats capsized. Another wreck lies buried at the northern end of the beach. A ship carrying a vast quantity of silver coins was wrecked on the beach in the late 17th century. The hulk of this 'dollar ship' was exposed in the early 19th century and many coins were found by villagers. A ghost in a black coach pulled by four grey horses is said to haunt the bay. Excavations in 1979 on the terrace above the beach exposed the remains of a building and a church dating about 1150. It is thought that severe storms may have buried the buildings with sand, forcing the villagers to move to the top of the cliffs.

Worms Head. This narrow one mile long neck of land is connected to the mainland by a causeway which is exposed at low tide. The name comes from Orm or Wurm and means sea

Walking on Rhossili Down

serpent or dragon. It is a nature reserve and guillemots and razorbills breed on the cliff ledges. Between the middle and outer heads there is a natural rock bridge known as the Devil's Bridge. The outer head has a blowhole which produces roaring sounds that can be heard more than a mile away. Anyone wishing to visit should check tide times and leave the Worm for the mainland not later than three and a half hours before the next high water (access across the rocks is two and a half hours either side of low tide).

St Mary's Church. The present church was built in the 13th century to replace the earlier one near the beach when it was engulfed by sand. It has a late Norman doorway and a saddleback tower. Inside there is a memorial to Edgar Evans who died on Captain Scott's expedition to the South Pole in 1912.

Rhossili Down. Rising to 632 feet above sea level, the summit is the highest point on Gwyr. It is a superb viewpoint , and is also

Worm's Head

rich in archaeological remains. The most conspicuous are the two Neolithic burial chambers known as Sweyne's Howes on the gentle eastern flank of the hill. About 100 metres north of the summit is a Bronze Age ring cairn with upright stones and a level platform. Another feature to look out for is the remains of a Second World War radar station.

Old Rectory. The vicar of Rhossili Church was also the vicar for the parish of Llangennith, so the rectory was built at the halfway point between the two parishes. The present house was built in 1850 and is now owned by the National Trust.

Burry Holms. This small limestone island lies at the northern end of Rhossili Bay and it is only accessible at low tide. An Iron Age promontory fort bisects the island. Excavations carried out in the 1960s discovered a tiny 12th century stone church in an oval enclosure, 12th century houses and a medieval hall house.

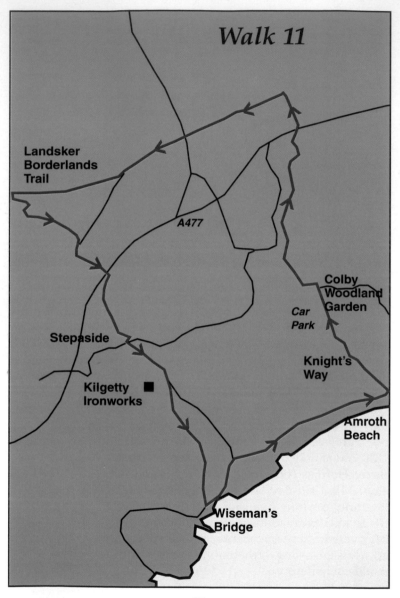

Walk 11

Landsker
Borderlands
Trail

A477

Colby
Woodland
Garden

Car
Park

Stepaside

Knight's
Way

Kilgetty
Ironworks

Amroth
Beach

Wiseman's
Bridge

II. COLBY WOODLAND GARDEN
Tel: 01834 811885

Colby Woodland Garden

An industrialist called John Colby built Colby Lodge in 1803. At that time the valley was being mined for anthracite and iron ore. About 100 years later, Major Kay from Stockport bought the Colby Estate and he planted the woodland garden, partly with rhododendrons his brother had acquired in the Himalayas. His descendants improved the gardens, and the estate remained in the Kay family until 1965, when the lodge and part of the estate was sold to Mr Peter Chance. Major Kay's granddaughter, Miss Mason, retained the woodland garden and gave it to the National Trust at the time of her death in 1979. Five years later, Mr Chance gave the part of the estate he had acquired to the National Trust. Colby is known for it beautiful, informal gardens, rhododendrons, woodland walks and tranquillity.

Beach at Wiseman's Bridge

Colby Woodland Garden

The walk – *goes inland on The Knights Way then leaves it for some quiet country lanes, and a short stretch of the Landsker Borderlands Trail before descending through Stepaside to Wiseman's Bridge. The Pembrokeshire Coast Path is followed to Amroth, where The Knights Way leads back to the start.*

8 miles – 4-5 hours

Start at the car park at Colby Woodland Garden, Amroth. Buses run to Amroth, which is on the route, from Tenby.

From the car park, go out to the lane and turn left. Cross a bridge and continue along the lane. On reaching a bridleway sign, ignore the first track on the right but, after a couple of metres, take another track on the right with a bridleway sign and **The Knights Way** waymark.

Have a stream on your left and go through a gate to follow the track through the wood. Ignore paths on the left and walk uphill to a gate, and emerge on a wider track. Turn left to pass a farmhouse and go slightly right to join a drive. It swings to the right and, after a gate, leave it to go left on a track to the A477.

Cross the road with care to a lane (Rosemary Lane) and follow it to houses. Bear left with the lane (leaving The Knights Way) and walk downhill. Turn right at a lane junction and ignore a lane on the right to Tavernspite. After a couple of metres, go left along a narrow lane.

Pass Blackmoor Cottage and the drive to Blackmoor Farm on your right. After about another 100 metres, go right on a track with a bridleway sign and the **Landsker Borderlands Trail** waymark. When the track bends right to a field, go left on a path that leads to a bridle-gate and field.

Walk through the long field to a gate in the far left corner. Turn right on a track to a lane, then bear left to a lane junction. Turn right and cross a bridge over the A477.

Walk downhill to **Stepaside** and turn right on a road with a sign for Wiseman's Bridge and Pleasant Valley. Go under a road bridge and walk along the pavement, passing the remains of

Amroth Beach

The Knight's Way waymark

Kilgetty Ironworks on your right.

Turn right on a track signed 'To Coast Path'. Follow it through the trees and ignore any paths leading off. It follows the route of a disused tramway. Join a lane and turn left to **Wiseman's Bridge.**

Turn left over the bridge and pass Wiseman's Bridge Inn. Walk uphill and ignore a lane on the left. After about another 100 metres, turn right onto a 'no through road' and, at its end, pass through a gate to continue along a track. You are now walking along the Pembrokeshire Coast Path. Go through a kissing-gate on the right and bear left downhill on a clear path to a stile. Continue downhill through the woods and emerge near the beach in **Amroth.**

With the sea on your right, follow the road for about 200 metres, then turn left on a lane. Walk uphill and after 150 metres, go left on a private road that has a footpath sign. Follow the tree lined track to a junction and ignore a path on the right. After a few more metres, bear right to Colby Woodland Garden.

OTHER POINTS OF INTEREST
The Knights Way. The trail links places connected with the Knights Templar and Knights Hospitaller between Blackpool Bridge on the Eastern Cleddau and Amroth. The Knights Templar were founded in the early 12th century to protect pilgrims in the Holy Land, and they were exempt from all authority apart from the Pope's. They received large donations of land and money. The Knights Hospitaller, also known as The Order of the Hospital of Saint John of Jerusalem, originated as a monastic brotherhood caring for the needs of pilgrims. At one time the church in Amroth was in their care.

Landsker Borderlands Trail. This is a 60 mile circular walk from Whitland. The word landsker is Norse for frontier. When the Normans arrived in Pembrokeshire in the mid 11th century, they built fortresses and established colonies in the south of Pembrokeshire, driving out the Welsh. This part of Pembrokeshire later became known as 'Little England Beyond Wales'. The Landsker marks the division between Welsh speaking north Pembrokeshire and the English speaking south.

Stepaside. The village of Stepaside grew around two local properties known as Stepaside. It lies above anthracite coal measures, and iron ore is also found in the area. According to a local story, the name is derived from Oliver Cromwell who, on his march in Pembrokeshire in 1648, told his men to 'step aside' and refresh themselves with a meal at this point.

Kilgetty Ironworks. The ironworks opened in 1848, and the ore

Kilgetty Ironworks

Landsker Borderlands Trail

was obtained mainly from levels driven in the cliffs between Amroth and Saundersfoot. The Grove Colliery, on the hill above, provided coal for the works. The iron works closed in 1877.

Wiseman's Bridge. In 1943, rehearsals for D-day landings were held on the beach at Wiseman's Bridge. Winston Churchill, the then Prime Minister, and high ranking officers of the British and Allied forces watched the event.

Amroth. Now a pleasant, small seaside resort, Amroth was once a mining village known for its high quality coal. Neolithic flints have been found on the beach. At low tide it is sometimes possible to see the tree stumps of a forest submerged by rising

Wiseman's Bridge

sea levels at the end of the last Ice Age. There used to be a row
of cottages on the seaward side of the road, but they have been
washed away by storms. Standing on the site of an earlier
fortress, the present Amroth Castle is an 18th century castellated
house said to have been visited by Nelson on his tour of Wales
in 1802. Amroth marks the start of the Pembrokeshire Coast
Path (or the end for walkers starting at St Dogmaels).

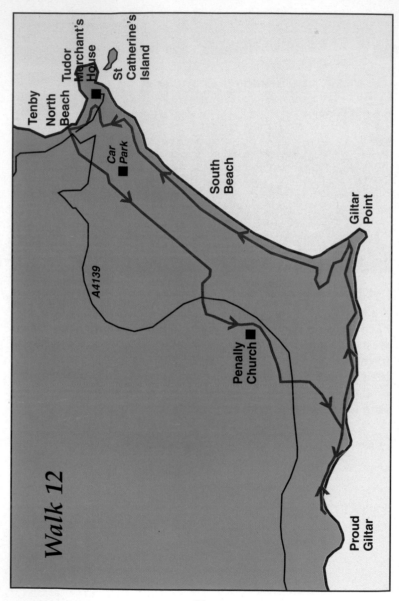

Walk 12

Tenby North Beach

Tudor Merchant's House

St Catherine's Island

Car Park

A4139

South Beach

Giltar Point

Penally Church

Proud Giltar

94

12. Tudor Merchant's House
Tel: 01834 842279

The Tudor Merchant's House

This late 15th century house is thought to be the oldest house in Tenby. A tall three-storied building, with furniture of later periods, it recreates what a prosperous merchant's house would have been like when the town was a busy port. The house has interesting architectural features, including a Flemish chimney, garderobes and also a small herb garden.

The walk – *after a short exploration of Tenby, the route takes you to the pleasant village of Penally, then joins the Pembrokeshire Coast Path and returns along the scenic cliff path and South Beach. A section of cliff path is in the Penally Range and it is closed when firing takes place. To check the operation dates, phone 01834 845595.*
6 miles – 3-4 hours

Caldey Island Ferry

Caldey Island from the Cliffs

Start the walk at Tenby's South Beach car park. If using public transport (trains or buses), start the walk at the Five Arches (the south-west gate) in the old town walls.

From the car park, walk towards the beach and bear left to pass in front of the café. Follow a zigzag path uphill to the top of the cliffs. Enjoy views of **Caldey Island** and **St Catherine's Island** on your right. Walk along the Esplanade and, at its end bear left to walk into the centre of **Tenby.** Ignore the first arch in the town wall on your right. Pass a square tower and a D shaped tower, then go right through the **Five Arches** to the end of the road. Turn left and pass **St Mary's Church,** then

North Beach

bear right. After a few metres, go left down Quay Hill to the Tudor Merchant's House.

With your back to the Tudor house, go left to the road running above **Tenby Harbour.** (Notice on your right, above the harbour, **Castle Hill.**) Bear left to the High Street and turn right to have views over North Beach. At the Royal Lion Hotel, turn left along White Lion Street and cross over a road to Warren Street. Pass St John's Methodist Church and cross a road to Edward Street. Ignore a road on the right.

At the end of the road, go right downhill and, after a few metres, go left along a lane signed Golf Course. A path joins it from the left. Walk straight ahead, passing Tenby Golf Club on your left.

With the golf course on your left, follow the track and pass a house to reach a track junction. Go ahead on a footpath and, at its end, cross the railway line and walk along a track to a road. Cross the road to a lane and walk along it to another road. Turn

Penally Church

left to **Penally Church** beside the Village Green. **St Deiniol's Well** is beside the lane that passes Penally Abbey Hotel.

Continue along the road and pass two pubs, the village hall and a caravan site. Immediately after passing the site, go left through a kissing-gate and walk through a field to another kissing-gate and the main road. Cross the road to a track and follow it under the railway bridge to a small gate and the Penally Range.

Walk uphill beside the right-hand fence to the cliff top. The walk turns left here, but it is worthwhile to follow the path right for a few hundred metres to have views of **Proud Giltar** and the coastline further west.

Return to the range and, assuming no red flags are flying and it is safe to continue, walk along the cliff path and go through a small gate. From here are superb views of **Caldey Island** and **St Margaret's Island**.

Go through another gate and follow the cliff path. After passing Giltar Point, you will have views on your right of Tenby's South Beach and the town of Tenby. The path goes downhill through trees to the beach. Walk along it to the café and car park at the start of the walk.

OTHER POINTS OF INTEREST

Caldey Island. The English name is a legacy from the Viking invasion of this part of Wales – *keld* (spring) and *ey* (island). The Welsh name Ynys Bŷr refers to the missionary Pyro who established a community on the island in the sixth century. He was followed by St Samson who became the first Bishop of Dol in Brittany. It is rumoured that the Celtic monks may have been killed by the Vikings.

A priory was founded on the island in the early 12th century under the abbey of St Dogmaels near Aberteifi *(Cardigan)*. After the dissolution of the monasteries, followed by several changes of ownership, Reverend Bushell purchased Caldey Island in 1897 and did some restoration work on the priory and churches. Benedictine monks came to the island in 1906 and built the modern abbey. Twenty-two years later they moved to Prinknash near Gloucester. Cistercian monks from Belgium took over and this strict community now produces world famous perfumes from the island's flowers. There are boat trips to Caldey Island during the summer months.

Proud Giltar and Lydstep Haven

St Catherine's Island. On top of the island is a fort built AD 1869 as part of a defensive scheme for the protection of Milford Haven. It was built to meet the threat of a French invasion that never materialised.

Tenby. A poem about Tenby was composed about AD 875 by Taliesin, the Celtic bard. Called 'Etmic Dinbych (in English it means 'In praise of the little fort') it describes the place now known as Tenby and those who lived there. It is thought that this is how the town acquired its name and, over the centuries, Dinbych has been anglicized into Tenby. It is now called in Welsh, Dinbych-y-pysgod which, translated into English, means 'Little Fort of the Fishes'.

The Norman invasion in the 11th century led to the capture of Tenby and, after a period of conflict, the town grew into a prosperous port. Then, in the mid 17th century, came the Civil War followed by a plague that killed many of the citizens, after which the town declined.

St. Margaret's Island and Caldey Island

Tenby Harbour

In the mid 18th century, visits to the seaside became an accepted cure for wealthy invalids. At Tenby, new properties were built, including a development with bathing machines and entertainments. The resort became very fashionable and after the arrival of the railway in the 1860s, Tenby became accessible to more visitors. Today, the town with its beautiful sandy beaches is one of the most popular seaside resorts in Wales.

Five Arches. The Norman walls were built in the late 13th century by the Earl of Pembroke. The original walls were only 15 feet high and the entry was a single arch. The barbican and the D shaped towers north of the gate were added in the 14th century. Jasper Tudor refortified the walls a century later. The moat, that was present then, was widened to 30 feet, and the walls heightened with higher arrow slits and a new parapet walk. The additional arches in the gate were knocked through in the 19th century.

St Mary's Church. The church dates from the end of the 13th century, but was greatly enlarged in the 15th century due to the prosperity of the town. The building has a 152 feet steeple, decorative features and interesting monuments. There are tombs from the early 15th century, including those of Thomas and John White. Thomas White hid the 14 years old Henry Tudor after the Battle of Tewkesbury and he also helped in his escape to Brittany. After his return to Pembrokeshire in 1485, Henry Tudor marched with supporters to Bosworth where he defeated King Richard 111 in the Battle of Bosworth, and was crowned Henry V11, the first Tudor King.

A tablet memorial in the church records that Dr Robert Recorde, a mathematician and Royal physician who invented the equality sign (=), was born in Tenby in 1510.

Tenby Harbour. Between the 14th and 16th centuries, Tenby grew into a busy port, importing fruit and wine from Portugal, Spain and France as well as horses and timber from Ireland and household goods from Devon. The first oranges to arrive in Wales were landed in Tenby in 1566 from Aveiro in Portugal.

The Five Arches

The Tudor Merchant's House

Tenby exported coal, wool, fish, and oysters. Close to the harbour is St Julien's Chapel, the 'Fisherman's Church'.

Castle Hill. There was probably a Celtic fort here before the Normans took Tenby in the early 12th century and built a keep on the hill. The stronghold was captured by the Welsh in 1153. A barbican was built in the early 13th century and watchtowers later on. The castle fell into disrepair, but Tenby saw action during the Civil War when the town and castle was held for the Parliamentarians. In 1648, a unit of Royalists held the castle for over two months, until forced to surrender because of a lack of food.

Penally Church. During medieval times, Penally was on the pilgrims' route to St David's. St Teilo, who became the first Bishop of Llandaff, was born in Penally. The present church dates from the Norman period, and is now dedicated to St Nicholas and St Teilo. Inside are two elaborately carved crosses that once stood in the churchyard. The church contain a 13th century tomb with an old French inscription.

St Deiniol's Well. St Deiniol is usually associated with northern Wales. He founded a church at Bangor, in Gwynedd, about AD 525 and was consecrated Bishop. The cathedral at Bangor is dedicated to him, as well as several other churches and, it is thought, there was probably once a chapel dedicated to St Deiniol opposite this well.

Proud Giltar. On this headland are blowholes connected to deep caves. From here are views of the beach at Lydstep Haven, which is backed by a caravan park. The headland across the bay is Lydstep Point, owned by the National Trust since 1936. It is a breeding site for seabirds such as razorbill, guillemot and fulmar.

St Margaret's Island. This tiny island was once connected to Caldey Island by a causeway. During the 19th century, people lived on St Margaret's Island and worked in the limestone quarries there. It is now a nature reserve with a large cormorant colony and where other birds, such as kittiwakes and razorbills, breed.

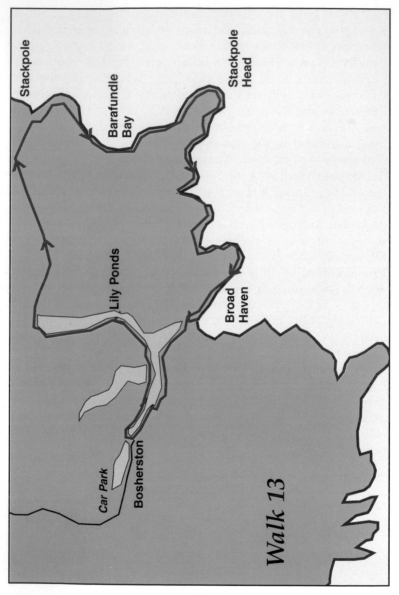

Stackpole

Barafundle
Bay

Stackpole
Head

Lily Ponds

Broad
Haven

Car Park

Bosherston

Walk 13

13. Bosherston Lily Ponds

Causeway across Lily Pond

The lily ponds are part of the Stackpole Estate which, from 1689 to 1976 was owned by the Campbells, Earls of Cawdor. John Campbell built a new mansion, Stackpole Court, about 1735 and established a walled garden which produced many kinds of fruit. After inheriting the estate in 1777, his grandson landscaped on a large scale, creating a deer park and damming what was to become the eastern arm of the lake. Formed in the last Ice Age, the narrow, limestone valleys were tidal reefs until they were dammed. More improvements were carried out in the 1860s and another dam was built, creating the other ponds. Part of the estate was taken by the War Office in 1938-1939 for the Castlemartin Range and Stackpole Court was used as barracks. The house had to be demolished in 1963 and the lands were sold whilst the remainder of the estate, including the lakes, passed to the National Trust. The lily

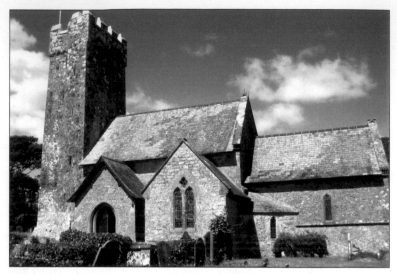

Bosherston Church

ponds are at their best in June and July, and are a good place for watching birds in the winter.

The walk – *follows paths beside the lily ponds, then heads to Stackpole Quay, and returns along the Pembrokeshire Coast Path, taking in beautiful Barafundle Bay.*
7 miles – 4 hours

Start at the car park in Bosherston village, off the B4319, south of Pembroke. Buses run to Bosherston (Coastal Cruiser) from Pembroke.

From the car park, take a path downhill through trees to a path junction. Cross the causeway over the lily pond and continue along a path. A short diversion on the right leads to a fine viewpoint. The path then descends to a footbridge over Central Arm and arrives at a footpath signpost. Turn right and ignore a stone bridge on the right.

Follow the level path along the Eastern Arm until you reach the Eight Arch Bridge. Cross it and go through a kissing-gate. Continue along the track (a permissive route) and cross over another track. Head downhill and go through a gate to the car park at **Stackpole Quay.**

Barafundle Beach

Walk through the car park and join a path that passes behind the tearoom. Go left to visit it, and Stackpole Quay. Return to the path and go through a gap in the wall to climb the stepped path that passes above the quay. Go through a kissing-gate and follow the clear path straight ahead. After veering to the right, it goes through an archway and descends steps to the beach at **Barafundle Bay**.

Cross the sandy beach to the other side, then take a path that rises through the trees to a kissing-gate. Follow the cliff path to **Stackpole Head** and, further on, go through a kissing-gate. After passing Raming Hole and Sand Pit, go through another kissing-gate to walk around Saddle Point, passing above **Broad Haven** beach.

Follow the path through a left-hand kissing-gate, and go up then down a sandy hill to a path junction near a footpath signpost. Turn left, but do not take the footpath to the beach (unless you want to visit it). Cross a smaller bridge and, continuing along the path, you will soon have a lily pond on your right. After passing an old brick building, you will reach the path junction met earlier. Turn left and retrace your steps to the car park. Before leaving the village, you may like to look at **Bosherston Church.**

Coastal Scenery

Lily Pond

OTHER POINTS OF INTEREST

Stackpole Quay

Stackpole Quay. The quay was built in the 18th century for exporting limestone from the nearby quarry. Coal and other goods were imported for the Campbell family who lived at Stackpole Court.

Barafundle Bay. Now owned by the National Trust, this lovely beach is part of the Stackpole Estate.

Stackpole Head. Razorbills, guillemots and fulmars breed here, and choughs may be seen. Look out for the blowholes (collapsed roofs of sea caves) through which the sea spouts during gales.

Broad Haven. Above the beach is Stackpole Warren which stretches as far as Barafundle Bay. Rabbits were bred for the estate. Offshore is a solitary rock known as Church Rock. This would be the pillar described in the Viking name of the estate – stac, an isolated pillar, and pollr, a small inlet.

Bosherston Church. The church is dedicated to St Michael and All Angels. Dating from the late 13th century, the building is on the site of a former church. Much restoration work took place in the mid 19th century, but there is a Norman font and two ancient tombs. A preaching cross stands in the churchyard.

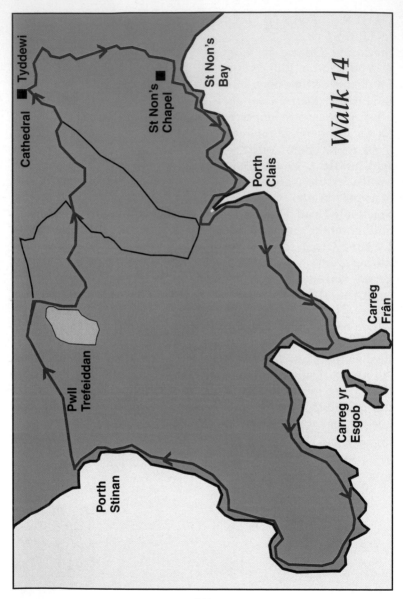

Walk 14

Cathedral ■ ■ Tyddewi

St Non's
Chapel ■

St Non's
Bay

Porth
Clais

Carreg
Frân

Carreg yr
Esgob

Pwll
Trefeiddan

Porth
Stinan

14. St David's Visitor Centre

Tel: 01437 720385

St. David's Visitor Centre

Located in the tiny city of St David's, the visitor centre has a shop and an interactive guide to the many National Trust properties in the area.

The walk – *from the centre of St David's, the route heads towards the sea and joins the Pembrokeshire Coast Path at St Non's Bay. A superb stretch of the coastal path is followed to Porth Stinan, from where the walk returns to the start via lanes and footpaths.*
10 miles – 5-6 hours

Start at the National Trust Visitor Centre in the High Street. There are several car parks in St David's. Buses run from Fishguard and Haverfordwest.

With your back to the Visitor Centre, go right for about 80

Medieval Preaching cross

metres, then bear right along a path called Y Gudel. Emerge in Bryn Road and turn right for 100 metres. Go left along Pen y Garn to its end. Turn right on a footpath for a few metres, then go left on a path signed St Non's.

Follow the enclosed path through several gates until it enters a field. Keep to the left side of it and go through a gate. Across to your right is a chapel at St Non's Retreat. Walk downhill to the cliff path. There are two footpaths nearby on your right.

Porth Clais

Porth Stinan

Take the nearer path and follow it to **St Non's Well.** Go through a gate into a field where, in an enclosure, is the ruined **St Non's Chapel.** Cross the field on a clear path to stone steps in a wall and join the coastal path.

Bear right along the path, which winds above coves to **Porth Clais.** Ignore the first path on the left, but take the next one and descend to the harbour. Turn right to a road, and bear left over a bridge.

Turn left on a path that rises above limekilns and gives good views of the harbour. After going through a gate, follow the main (right-hand) path. As you continue along the path, you will see the rocky off-shore islets called Carreg Frân and Carreg yr Esgob. The path descends to the beach in Porthlysgi Bay.

Bear right for a few paces, then climb up again on another path. You will soon reach a fork, where you go left up the steep hill and through a small gate. The path climbs over rocks, and you will see pools ahead near cottages. Descend slightly above

Ramsey Island

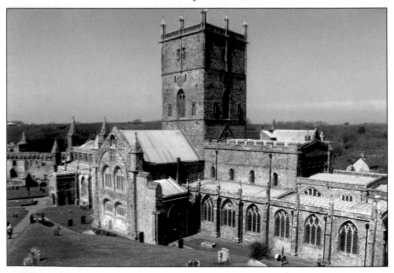

St. David's Cathedral

Porth Henllys and ignore a path on the right.

The path climbs to a small gate, and goes uphill and around a headland through heather and gorse to have great views ahead of **Ramsey Island**. Pass through a small gate and continue along the coastal path. With Ramsey Island soon on your left, this is a beautiful stretch of the walk.

Continue along the coastal path, ignoring paths leading off, until you reach the lifeboat station at **Porth Stinan**. Leave the coast path here, and turn right along a lane.

Pass farms on your left and right, and take the first lane on the right, to pass Pwll Trefeiddan on your right. At a left bend, ignore a footpath on the right and, after about another 200 metres, go left along a track.

Pass buildings and follow the track as it bears right to meet another track. Bear left to a lane and turn left downhill. After 150 metres, turn right on a track (bridleway). Pass a house and cross a stream, then pass more buildings. Continue to a broad gate with blue arrows, and follow the obvious, partly enclosed, track.

The path eventually bends right to pass houses and emerges on a road. Turn left and, after 200 metres, go left downhill on a road to a junction. Cross the road, slanting left, to a lane signed pedestrians.

Walk along the lane to a junction, where you can go ahead to visit **St David's Cathedral**, or left to the **Bishop's Palace**.

To return to the start of the walk, turn right, bending left above the cathedral, and go through the gateway Porth y Tŵr to the crossroads, war memorial garden and the medieval preaching cross in St David's.

OTHER POINTS OF INTEREST
St Non's Well. The spring is said to have sprung forth immediately after St David was born, and it is dedicated to his mother. For hundreds of years, it was regarded as a holy well. Pins and coins were thrown in the well as an offering, especially on St Non's Day, 2 March. The stone vault dates from the 18th

St. Non's Chapel

century, and it may replace an earlier structure.

St Non's Chapel. According to legend, St David was born about AD 500 on the site of the ruined chapel. His mother was Non, a daughter of the Prince of Pembroke. During a thunderstorm, she was being pursued, whilst in labour, by King Sant of Cardigan, David's father. She gave birth at this place and a brilliant flash of lightning occurred as he was born. The ruined chapel dates from c.1300, and a 7th to 9th century incised stone stands in one of the corners. The chapel at St Non's Retreat was built in the 1930s.

Porth Clais. St David was baptised here by St Albeus (Elvis), an Irish bishop, Cargoes were brought to Porth Clais for the cathedral in the 14th century and, in later centuries, it became a busy trading port. Coal, timber and limestone were landed at the harbour. The limekilns on the quay have been restored.

Ramsey Island. The island is now a nature reserve owned by the RSPB. Birds such as guillemot, razorbill, fulmar, kittiwake,

St. Non's Well

chough and peregrine nest there. Seabirds in Ramsey Sound feed on the fish brought to the surface by the rushing tide. Seals breed there in the autumn. In early times, the island was owned by the Bishop of St David's, and from the 12th century it was let out to farmers. There were two chapels, one dedicated to St Derynog, and the other to St Stinan. Born in Brittany in the 6th century, St Stinan became a priest and came as a missionary to Wales. He lived on Ramsey Island and was a strict disciplinarian. One day his followers decided they could not take any more, and pushed him to the ground, then beheaded him. A spring of holy water issued from the spot where his head fell. St Stinan's decapitated body picked up the head, and walked across the waters of Ramsey Sound to the mainland, where he was buried at the place now called St Justinan.

Porth Stinan. This little harbour is also known as St Justinan, and is named after the 6th century saint who lived on Ramsey Island. The 16th century ruined chapel is said to mark his burial

The Bishop's Palace

place. The lifeboat station was built in 1911. In the summer, there are boat trips from the harbour to Ramsey Island.

St David's Cathedral. St David, the patron saint of Wales, founded a religious community in the 6th century. Living in this hollow, David and his monks led a spartan life and used no animals to work the land. They ate no meat, and drank only water. David has often been referred to as Dewi Ddyfrwr (David, the Water Drinker). The Celtic community became an important Welsh monastery, but no buildings remain from this period. After the Norman conquest, the religious settlement was reorganised to a different type of monasticism. The first Norman church at St David's was destroyed by fire, and the present building dates from the late 12th century. The nave is from this period, but the Norman roof has been replaced with an oak ceiling. Chapels have been added, and much restoration work has been carried out over the centuries. St David's Cathedral has been a place of pilgrimage since a medieval pope decreed that two journeys to St David's equalled one to Rome.

The Bishop's Palace. The first accommodation for bishops at St David's was probably small and basic. In the late 13th century, grander buildings were constructed, including a gatehouse, hall, apartments for the bishop and accommodation for guests. By the time Henry de Gower was elected bishop in 1328, St David's was a wealthy estate. He rebuilt the palace in an opulent, decorated style, which took until 1350 to complete. It remained until 1536, when Bishop Barlow decided the bishop's residence should be moved to Carmarthen. By the end of the 11th century, the palace was derelict.

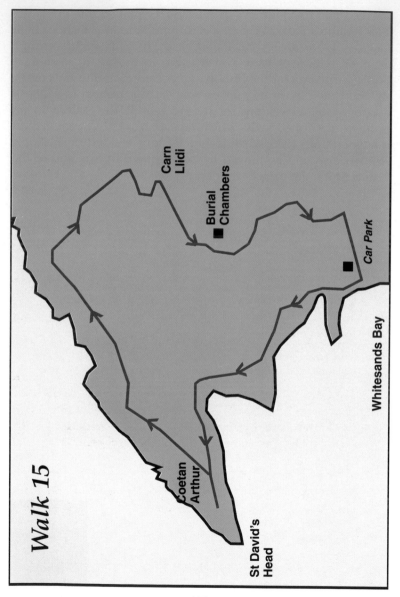

Walk 15

Carn Llidi

Burial Chambers

Car Park

Whitesands Bay

Coetan Arthur

St David's Head

15. St David's Head

Carn Llidi from St. David's Head

This famous, rugged headland was formed by volcanic activity about 500 million years ago. The Romans called it the Promontory of the Eight Perils. Much of the peninsula is covered in lowland heath, which is now an internationally rare habitat. The area is rich in archaeological remains.

The walk – *after following the Pembrokeshire Coast Path to the promontory of St David's Head, the route takes a further stretch of coast path, then climbs the shoulder of Carn Llidi, and returns along its scenic ridge.*
4 miles – about 3 hours

Carn Llidi Burial Chamber

Start at Whitesands Bay car park, two miles north-west of St David's on the B4583. There is a bus service from St David's to Whitesands Bay.

At the car park, face **Whitesands Bay**, and turn right along the coast path. It has an acorn symbol. Follow the main path and, after about 50 metres, you will pass a mound on your left which was the site of **St Patrick's Chapel**.

The path soon passes above cliffs and goes through a kissing-gate. Continue along the main path and descend to a stream. Cross a footbridge above Porthmeigan and follow the path left to the stone ramparts of **St David's Head Iron Age Fort.**

From the end of the headland are views to Ramsey Island. Walk back through the ramparts and bear left along the coastal path. After a few paces, leave it to take a narrower path that passes above the path walked to the headland. Head towards a rocky outcrop, and have it on your left. You should soon see, on your left, the Neolithic burial chamber called **Coetan Arthur.**

Carn Llidi

At the burial chamber, keep the outcrops on your left, and follow a path that gradually climbs, whilst slanting left, to rejoin the coastal path. Turn right along it and walk uphill to a point offering great views in all directions. Follow the path, as it descends, and ignore a path on the right.

Continue along the coastal path and walk uphill. Ignore a path on the right and head downhill. After about 100 metres, when you are above a small inlet, you should see a small signpost with an acorn symbol and a YHA sign.

Turn right along the path for about 80 metres to a path junction. Turn left, and ignore a path on the left. Soon afterwards, there is a wall on the left.

Walk uphill to the top of the hill's shoulder, where you will have views of the other (south) side of Pembrokeshire's coast. At this point, turn right along a fairly level path. After walking for about 200 metres, join a broader path and turn left towards the summit of **Carn Llidi.** After 120 metres, where the main path

Coetan Arthur

turns right, you can take a path going ahead towards Carn Llidi's summit. (If you do not want to climb up to the ridge, bear right along the lower path until you join the concrete path near the two burial chambers in the main route's directions.)

Continuing along the main route, follow the path that soon veers left to join the ridge to the left of its steepest part. Here are good views of the countryside and coast to the east. From this point, a path skirts around the right side of the summit rocks to join a path on the western side of Carn Llidi.

Here, it is possible, by scrambling up the rocks, to reach the topmost point of Carn Llidi. Most people, however, are content to reach this slightly lower point where there are excellent views of the coast and countryside.

Follow a path along the ridge to a concrete path and continue along it, downhill, passing the **Carn Llidi Burial Chambers** on your left.

Head downhill and, after joining another path near a

St. David's Head Iron Age fort

National Trust sign, turn left to a stile at a gate. Walk downhill and, after passing a farm, bear right to emerge at a lane end. Turn left to a lane junction, and bear right to the start of the walk at the car park.

OTHER POINTS OF INTEREST
Whitesands Bay. The name in Welsh for this lovely bay is Porth Mawr *(big bay)*. Occasionally, at very low tides, the remains of a submerged forest are visible. During the Bronze Age, there was a track from Stonehenge in the south-west of England that ran via the Preselli Hills to this bay. From here, a boat carried traders to Ireland in their search for copper.

St Patrick's Chapel. The site of a 6th century chapel is marked by a concrete slab. Excavated in the 1920s, it is thought to have been a sailor's chapel used for prayers before and after voyages. Dedicated to St Patrick, it is one of several places where the saint is said to have taken his last voyage to Ireland.

Whitesands Beach and St David's Head

St David's Head Iron Age Promontory Fort. The fort is known as Clawdd-y-milwyr (Warrior's Dyke). It has an outer well preserved rampart of about 100 metres, with two lesser walls inside. The footings of six round stone houses are visible. It was partly excavated in 1898 and flints, glass beads and pottery were found. East of the promontory, the fields with low stone walls in the moorland may date from the time of the fort (about 500 BC). From the end of the headland are good views towards Ramsey Island (see Walk 14). West of the promontory, off-shore, are the perilous islets known as the Bishops and Clerks.

Coetan Arthur. This Neolithic burial chamber, with its huge capstone, dates from 4,000-3,000 BC. When built, the whole structure would have been covered with stones and earth. The name of the tomb means 'Arthur's Quoit', and it refers to the game of quoits said to have been played in this area by the legendary King Arthur.

Carn Llidi. Rising to 181 metres (594 feet), this rocky hill is the highest point on St David's peninsula. From its ridge and summit are superb views of the coast, and other rocky outcrops. During the 1914-1918 war, it was the site of a hydrophone station used for detecting submarines.

Carn Llidi Burial Chambers. Sited below rocks, just off the path, these two small Neolithic burial chambers were erected 4,000-3,000 BC. They are partly subterranean and have large capstones. Some of the side stones have fallen.

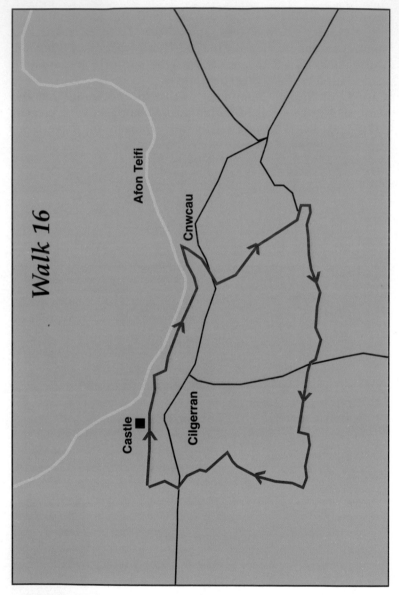

Walk 16

Afon Teifi

Cnwcau

Castle

Cilgerran

16. Cilgerran Castle
Tel: 01239 615007

The first castle built by the Normans at Cilgerran was probably a motte and bailey. The ruins we see today are the remains of a castle built in the 13th century. The earlier stronghold certainly had a turbulent history, and it may be the one from where Nest, the beautiful wife of Gerald de Windsor, ran away with Owain, son of Cadwgan, Prince of Powys, in 1109. The Lord Rhys captured Cilgerran Castle in 1164, but it was taken by William Marshall, Earl of Pembroke in 1204, only to be taken

Tower Cilgerran Castle

back by the Welsh in 1215 for Llewelyn ap Iorwerth. William Marshall's son, another William, recaptured the castle and he was probably responsible for the reconstruction.

The castle later became rather derelict, but was refortified in the 1370s because Edward 111 feared an invasion from France. Owain Glyndŵr is said to have held Cilgerran for a brief period in 1405. Henry V11 granted the castle to the Vaughan family, and they occupied it until the early 17th century. The stronghold then fell into ruin. From the 18th century it became fashionable for tourists to take boat trips from Aberteifi to view the castle, and artists such as Turner and Richard Wilson created their dramatic paintings from boats on Afon Teifi. Owned by the National Trust since 1938, Cilgerran Castle is under the guardianship of Cadw.

The walk – *descends from the castle to Afon Teifi, and follows a riverside path before returning to the village through pleasant countryside.*
3.5 miles – 2 hours

Cilgerran Castle above Afon Teifi

Cilgerran Stone

Start at Cilgerran Castle, which is close to the centre of Cilgerran. The village is south of Aberteifi *(Cardigan)*, off the A478. There are buses to Cilgerran from Aberteifi.

Face the castle entrance and take a track on the right. Follow it to a footpath signpost near a house then bear left downhill on a path to another signpost. Go right down steps to the next signpost. Turn left to another signpost at a bend, and bear right then left to emerge on a broad track beside **Afon Teifi.**

Bear right along the track to a picnic area at the **National**

Coracle Centre. Continue on a path beside the river for about 800 metres, then take a track on the right signposted Village. It soon bends to the right and, higher up, passes between houses to emerge on a road in the village of Cnwcau.

Turn right to pass the Mason's Arms on your right, and bear left on a lane signposted Llwyncelyn. Pass houses and walk downhill to a left bend, where there is a house

Teifi Coracle

on the left. Bear right at a footpath signpost to take a path that descends a few steps. Go through a gate onto a path through trees and along a narrow boardwalk.

On reaching a footbridge, do not cross it, but climb a stile on the right. Follow the permissive path through the field by going ahead and uphill to a small gate on the left side of a house. Turn left to climb a stile at a gate and follow the right-hand boundary of a field to a corner, then go left to a stile at a gate on the right. Walk ahead to pass below a house. Before the end of this long field, bear right at a corner and, in a few paces, climb a stile in another corner.

Turn left along the access track to a stone stile at a gate, and emerge on a road. Turn right for about 60 metres, then climb a stile on the left. Walk beside the left-hand fence to a stile in the corner. After a few paces, cross a stile on the left onto an old track bordered by trees and shrubs.

After walking along the track for about 200 metres, ignore a stile on the right and climb the stile in front of you. Follow the track and, on reaching a house keep to the left to walk downhill on a grassy track. Ignore a field gate on the left and also, a little further on, a footpath on the left, and go through the field gate in front of you.

Bear right and, in a few metres, enter another field on the right. Slant uphill to the far top corner where there is a stile, and turn left on a track. It bears to the left, then to the right, to pass the embankments of the dismantled **Cardi-Bach Railway**. Emerge on a road in Cilgerran and cross it to a pavement. Turn left for about 30 metres, then bear right along an enclosed path and follow it to a small gate giving access to the churchyard of **Cilgerran Church**.

Pass the church on your right and bear right through the churchyard to Church Street. Turn right and follow the road to Castle Square, near the start of the walk.

OTHER POINTS OF INTEREST

Afon Teifi. The river has its source in the southern Cambrian Mountains, near the Teifi Pools, north of Tregaron. It flows through Lampeter, Llandysul, Newcastle Emlyn, Cenarth and Aberteifi before it reaches Cardigan Bay at Gwbert. Afon Teifi is tidal as far as the bridge at Llechryd, a couple of miles upriver from Cilgerran. In the mid 18th century there was an ironworks at Llechryd, and iron ore was shipped up the river for processing. Tin plate, slates and dairy produce were exported. The river is rich in wildlife and heron, kingfisher and dipper may be seen from the riverbank.

National Coracle Centre. Coracles are bowl shaped boats designed for fishing on swiftly flowing rivers. The Romans described them being used by Celtic tribes in Britain. The word 'coracle' comes from the Welsh 'cwrwgl'. Various types are used in other parts of the world, including the curragh in Ireland. At one time they were used on most Welsh rivers, but today they are restricted to the rivers Teifi, Tywi and Taf.

Coracles have been used on Afon Teifi since time immemorial, and at Cigerran they were used for ferrying people across the river as well as fishing. The framework is made of willow strips with hazel plaits for the gunwale. Hide was the original covering for the coracle, but since the early 19th century calico or a similar material waterproofed with pitch has been used. The coracle has to be light enough to carry to and from the river. It is manoeuvred by describing a rough figure of eight with the ash paddle. The method of catching fish on Afon Teifi was for two coracles to be paddled downstream, one beside each bank, with a long weighted net strung between them. In the mid 19th century there were more than 300 coracles used on the river, and most cottages had one hanging by the door.

The 1923 Salmon and Freshwater Fisheries Act prohibited coracle fishing on many rivers. Coracles now have to be licensed, and the number is limited because of the use of nets. A coracle regatta takes place every August in Cilgerran.

Cardi-Bach Railway. This railway line, known affectionately as the Cardi-Bach, operated between Aberteifi *(Cardigan)* and Whitland from 1886 to 1982.

Cilgerran church. The church is dedicated to St Llawddog who lived in the 6th century. He is said to have performed miracles, and his festival day is 15 January. The church has a 13th century tower, but otherwise dates mainly from the 19th century. In the churchyard (to the right of the path, in the second row) is a 6th century stone with Ogham and Latin inscriptions, which translates: 'Here lies Trenegussus the son of Macutrenus'.

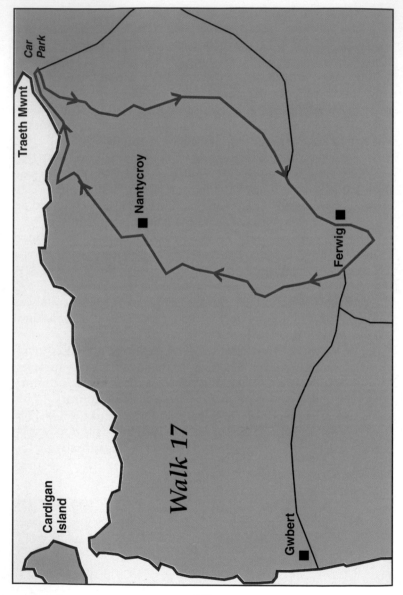

Car
Park

Traeth Mwnt

Nantycroy

Ferwig

Walk 17

Cardigan
Island

Gwbert

134

17. Mwnt

Church of the Holy Cross, Mwnt

Mwnt is a beautiful, remote spot on the Ceredigion Heritage Coast. There is a small, sandy beach below a massive headland. The Flemings landed here in 1155 and were defeated by the Welsh. Until about 200 years ago, the victory was commemorated every January by a games meeting called Sul Coch y Mwnt (Bloody Sunday of the Mound).

The walk – *tracks and lanes to Y Ferwig, returning by a farm lane, track and cliff path with fine coastal views.*
5 miles – 2-3 hours

Beach, Mwnt

Start at the National Trust car park above Mwnt Beach. Mwnt is north-east of Aberteifi *(Cardigan)*, off the A487, signposted from Penparc. Buses run from Aberteifi to Y Ferwig (on the route).

At the car park, face the tiny **Church of the Holy Cross**. Behind the church is the headland known as **Foel y Gwynt**. Turn left along the road and, in a few metres, go right along a track. At the toilets, ignore a path on the right that goes downhill to the beach.

Cross a level bridge over a stream and walk uphill, passing an old limekiln on the right. Stay on the main path and go through a gate across it. Walk uphill until you see a footpath signpost pointing back the way you came. Ignore a path on the right and continue uphill. You will have a fence on your left and a house to the right. Go through a bridle gate and, in a few paces, walk ahead on a track.

The track becomes surfaced and rises above a valley. Emerge on another lane, and turn right to follow it to a road junction in

Duck Pond

the village of Y Ferwig. Turn right, ignore a lane on the left, and bear right uphill, passing houses.

On reaching a fork, take the right-hand lane, a 'no through road'. Pass Bolafron Farm and Penfiedr. The lane curves right and, after passing a duck pond, there are views of the sea. Pass Fferm Tyriet on the left and, when the lane bends right, ignore a track on the left. Walk ahead in the direction of Nant-y-Groi Farm.

Ignore a track on the right and walk downhill to pass through a gate across the track. Turn left between buildings and go through a gate on the right. Follow a hedged track. It bends to the right and, in places, there are views on the left of **Cardigan Island.**

The path becomes narrower and, at its end, go through a gate across it. Bear left beside the field boundary to a kissing-gate in the lower corner. Turn right along the cliff path to have a fence on your right. The path eventually leaves the fence and goes

Church of the Holy Cross

Foel y Wynt, Mwnt Church and beach

downhill through gorse and into a little valley.

Cross a level footbridge over a stream and walk uphill to another stretch of cliff path. It leads to a kissing-gate and, further on, rejoins the outward route near the limekiln. Retrace your steps to the start.

OTHER POINTS OF INTEREST
Church of the Holy Cross. The small whitewashed church dates from about the 14th century. It stands on an earlier Celtic site on the route to Ynys Enlli (Bardsey Island), the traditional burial place of saints. The church was also on the route to St David's. In the church is a 14th century font and old pieces of timber, with carvings of saints' heads, that once formed the rood screen.
Foel y Wynt. A cross once stood on top of this 250 foot steep headland. The slopes are a good vantage point for watching the Atlantic grey seals and bottle-nosed dolphins that visit the bay.
Cardigan Island. This small island lies about 100 metres from the mainland. It has been a nature reserve since 1944 and was purchased by the West Wales Naturalists' Trust in 1963. Herring gulls and other sea birds, including fulmar, nest on the cliffs. At one time there was a huge brown rat colony, but they were exterminated in the late 1960s.

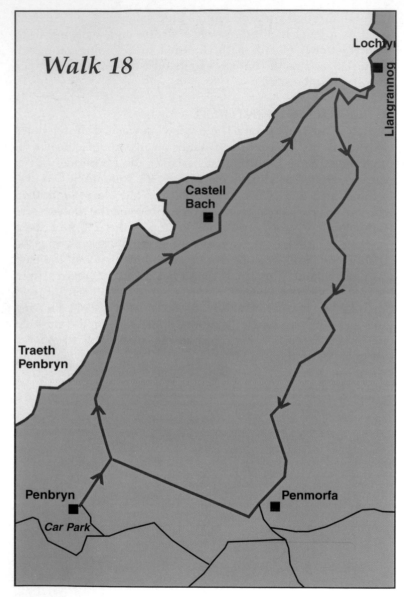

Walk 18

Lochtyr

Llangrannog

Castell
Bach

Traeth
Penbryn

Penbryn

Car Park

Penmorfa

18. Penbryn

Llangrannog Beach

The settlement of Penbryn lies in the peaceful, wooded valley of the Hoffnant, only a few hundred metres by lane from the sandy beach of Traeth Penbryn. It is said that, in the past, the beach and valley were frequented by smugglers. At low tide, the beach extends to Tre-saith and, according to local legend, seven Irish princesses landed on the beach after being cast adrift by their father in a boat without sails or oars. They married the richest farmers in the area.

The walk – *a scenic stretch of coastal path to the picturesque, seaside village of Llangrannog. The return is by lanes and a woodland path that rejoins the outward route above Penbryn.*
5 miles – about 3 hours

Llangrannog beach

Start at the National Trust car park at Llanborth Farm, Penbryn, accessed by lanes from Sarnau on the A487. There is a limited bus service to Llangrannog on the route. More frequent buses run from New Quay and Aberteifi *(Cardigan)* to Sarnau, two miles from the start.

From the car park, turn left to pass the café and a house on the left. At the end of the farm buildings on the right, go right through a gate onto a track signed Llangrannog, and join a track coming from the farm. Walk uphill to a footpath signpost and bear left. As you go uphill, look back at the views. Above Penbryn, surrounded by fields and woodlands, is **St Michael's Church.**

On reaching a gate across the track, go left through a kissing-gate and follow the path through bushes. After climbing a stile, continue along the left side of the field and, further on, go between bushes to a stile. Slant downhill to a stile in the lower right-hand corner of the field.

The path descends for a few paces, then bears to the right above a cove to a small gate. Climb up through gorse for a short distance, then descend the steep hill on a partly stepped path to a footbridge over a stream.

Climb the path to a stile then bear left beside a fence. Pass between bushes, then bear right with the sea now below on your left. After the path bends right, climb a stile on the left to continue along the cliff path, between bushes and a fence.

The path makes a gradual descent with views of the **Lochtyn** promontory beyond **Llangrannog**. The path leaves the fence and goes downhill through gorse and, after a stepped section, passes between hedges below a house to emerge on a lane, near a bend. Go left downhill along the lane to Llangrannog.

Penbryn Beach

After resting, leave the village by passing Pentre Arms on your left and walking uphill along the lane that you descended. Instead of taking the coastal path, follow the lane left at the bend, and climb the hill. After passing a long stretch of woodland, the lane emerges from the trees and passes a house and farm.

Pass a 'no through road' on your right and bear left with the lane. Follow it to a junction and turn right. Walk downhill and, about 60 metres after passing a chapel on the right, turn right at a footpath signpost and stile.

Walk ahead, slightly left, to a path entering bushes and go downhill to join another path. Continue with a field on the left and enter woodland. Have a stream below on your left and pass through a kissing-gate.

Follow a clear path until it joins a track. Turn right and ignore a track on the left, but walk ahead to pass a house on the left. Reach a footpath signpost and maintain your direction, then go through a gate and follow a path in the direction of the sea.

Pass through a gate to the footpath junction met earlier on the walk, and turn left downhill along the track to the start of the walk at Penbryn car park.

OTHER POINTS OF INTEREST

St Michael's Church. The church dates from the 12th century and has a circular churchyard. It is said that a wooden church once stood at this location, and a decision was made to build a stone church on another site. Every night, the stonework built

St Michael's Church

during the day was moved by inexplicable means to the old site. Eventually, it was decided to build the new church where it is now. The grave of Mrs Anne Adeliza Puddicombe, a romantic novelist, lies in the churchyard. She wrote under the name Allen Raine and her novels, written in the early 20th century, include 'A Welsh Witch' and 'Hearts of Wales'. She lived at Tresaith.

Lochtyn. At the end of the promontory is the rocky islet, Ynys Lochtyn. On the hill Pendinas Lochtyn, is an Iron Age hillfort. The walk to the promontory is a popular walk, and it was a favourite of the composer Edward Elgar, who had a holiday in Llangrannog in 1902. One day, whilst he was enjoying the view, and thinking about the theme for his Introduction and Allegro for Strings, he heard local people singing on the beach. Although the songs were indistinct, the sounds fitted his mood, enabling him to write his famous tune.

Llangrannog. The village grew from a religious community established by St Carantoc, a sixth century Celtic saint who built a church in the steep valley. The community worked at farming and fishing and, in the late 18th century, the sheltered cove became a port, importing limestone and household goods. A limekiln still stands above the beach. Small coasters were built on the shore, the largest being the 300 ton schooner called 'Anne and Catherine'. A prominent rock on the beach is Carreg Bica, the Devil's Tooth. According to local legend, the rock was a tooth belonging to the Devil. Because it was giving him agonising toothache, he pulled it out and flung it on Llangrannog Beach.

The Lochtyn Peninsula

Views from the coastal path

Penbryn

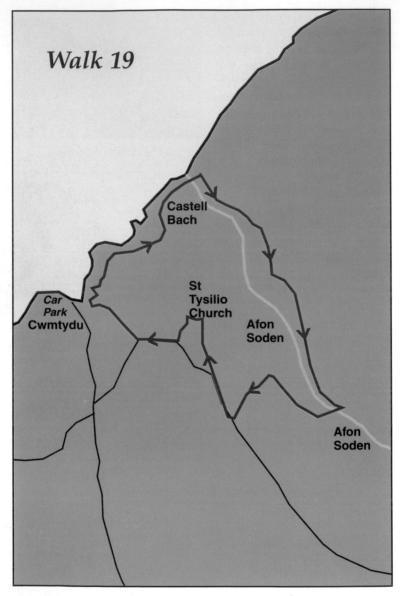

Walk 19

Castell
Bach

St
Tysilio
Church

Afon
Soden

*Car
Park*
Cwmtydu

Afon
Soden

19. Cwmtydu

The shingle beach at Cwmtydu with the old smugglers' cave in the rocks

Cwmtydu is a small cove with a shingle beach lying at the mouth of Afon Ffynnon Ddewi. The cove was used by smugglers in the 18th century for the landing of contraband, especially brandy from France and Ireland. The contraband was hidden in caves until it was safe to take it inland on horseback. At the back of the beach, there is an old limekiln, and it was used to burn limestone brought by boat from southern Wales. Local farmers used it to fertilize their land, collecting it from the kiln by horse and cart. The cliff path on Craig Caerllan, above the bay, is a good place to spot grey seals basking on the rocks. Porpoises and bottle-nosed dolphins may be spotted off-shore.

Church of St. Tysilio

The walk – *cliff paths, followed by woodland paths through a lovely, wooded valley, returning along lanes and passing the ancient church of St Tysilio.*
4 miles – 2-3 hours

Start at the car park above the beach at Cwmtydu, a small hamlet that lies a few miles south-west of New Quay. There is an infrequent bus service from Aberteifi *(Cardigan)* and Aberaeron to Caerwedros, one mile off-route.

At the car park, face the sea and turn right to go through a kissing-gate above the beach. Follow the coast path, which soon winds to the right, then to the left, and goes uphill to join another path. Turn left, but enjoy the south-west views, before descending above a rocky island to go through a kissing-gate onto the NT property, Pen y Graig.

At a public footpath signpost, ignore the sign and follow the coastal path to a broken wall above the cove. Go left and

Cliff path above Cwmtydu

continue on the path above the cliffs, passing through the Iron Age promontory fort, **Castell Bach**. Ignore a stepped path on the right, and take the path downhill to a kissing-gate. Go through it and cross a beach to a path on the other side of the cove.

Walk uphill to join another path and turn right to follow it above the lovely Afon Soden valley. After passing a meadow on the right, the path joins another at the NT sign Byrlip. Bear right and, after crossing a footbridge, turn left.

The path goes uphill and bears right to pass through a clearing, before entering trees. Go through a kissing-gate to leave the NT property, Cwm Soden. Follow the clear path through the trees and pass a field. The path passes above a beautiful, wooded valley to arrive at a fork. Take the right-hand path and follow it to a stile.

Climb the stile and turn left on a track. Go through a gate across the track and pass a house on the left. After a few paces,

Coastal Scenery

turn right on a lane to cross a small stone bridge. Walk uphill along the wooded lane and, after passing a farm, follow the lane as it bears left to a lane junction. Turn right and, when the lane bends left, leave it to walk along a 'no through road'.

Pass **St Tysilio Church** on your right and, after a few paces, go left through a kissing-gate. Walk along the right side of the field to another kissing-gate and turn left along a track. Go through a gate at a cattle grid and emerge on a lane. Turn right downhill to a fork, then bear right to follow the lane to the start at the car park.

OTHER POINTS OF INTEREST

Castell Bach. The name means Little Castle. This Iron Age promontory fort was probably occupied from the third century BC for approximately 400 years. The remains of its earth ramparts are still visible.

St Tysilio's Church. This 13th century church was rebuilt in

The limekiln near the car park at Cwmtydu

1825. The churchyard was originally circular, but it has been extended. An ancient stone-lined spring lies in a field to the north. The church is dedicated to St Tysilio who lived in the 7th century. He is said to be the son of Brochfael, a Prince of Powys, and he became a hermit on Church Island in the Menai Strait.

Cwmtydu

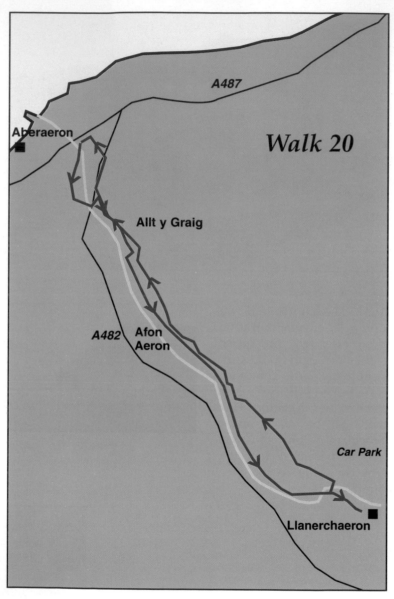

Walk 20

A487

Aberaeron

Allt y Graig

A482   Afon
         Aeron

Car Park

Llanerchaeron

20. LLANERCHAERON
Tel: 01545 570200

Llanerchaeron

Llanerchaeron is a captivating example of an 18th century Welsh country estate. The mansion was designed in the 1790s by the famous architect John Nash for William Lewis, and the estate stayed in the same family until John Powell Ponsonby Lewes bequeathed it to the National Trust in 1989. In the grounds of the Georgian country house there are walled gardens where fruit, vegetables, flowers and herbs are grown. The estate was self-sufficient, and visitors can look around the farm buildings. Today, the estate is worked as an organic farm.

Farm buildings in Llanerchaeron

The walk – *hillside and woodland paths, followed by lanes and pavements to the centre of Aberaeron, returning beside the river and along an old railway track. The route offers shorter options for those who do not want to walk as far as Aberaeron.*
5 miles – 2-3 hours (options of 2.5 or 3.5 miles – 1-2 hours)

Start at the car park on the opposite side of the lane to Llanerchaeron entrance gates. Llanerchaeron is signposted off the A482, south of Aberaeron. Buses from Aberystwyth to Carmarthen pass along the A482. An alternative start for the walk is Aberaeron, which is on several bus routes.

From the car park, go out into the lane and turn right. Pass **St Non's Church** on your left and, before the end of the churchyard, bear right through a gate into a field. Walk ahead and cross a bridge over Afon Aeron, and turn left on a path. After passing a small ruin on the right, the path veers away from the river, then goes downhill on a path bordered by trees.

Aberaeron Harbour

Emerge on a track and maintain your direction.

Pass farm buildings on the right, and climb a stile to follow a grassy track. Emerge on a farm access track and turn left. After a few paces, cross a stile on your right. Go ahead along the right boundary of the field to a small gate. Continue along the right-hand side of the next field but, at its end, veer left to a stile in trees, near a broad gate. Continue beside a fence to a stile and pass a ruin on your right.

Continue along the path and, after a few metres, veer to the right and follow a track between overgrown walls. The track descends, then levels and swings right towards a field. Bear left and walk through trees to a stile. On your left is the disused track of the **Aberaeron Branch Railway**. (The walk could be shortened at this point, by taking a path on your left to join the old railway track.)

To follow the longer walk, continue along the track you are already following, and walk uphill, with views on your left of

The Old Railway Track

the river. After having a field on the left, the track joins an access lane. Walk ahead to pass College Farm, then go downhill and, further along it, you will see a footpath signpost and steps on your right. (If you do not wish to walk all the way into Aberaeron, continue along the lane for another 40 metres, then bear left through a small car park to join the old railway track.)

To continue on the walk, go up the steps to Allt y Graig wood and, after joining another path, bear left. Pass an old quarry on your right and, at a fork, go left downhill to a kissing-gate and lane.

Turn right and ignore another lane on the right. Go downhill to the A482 and turn right for 200 metres into **Aberaeron**. When there is a Welsh Cob Stallion sculpture at a park on your left, turn left along Alban Square to a junction and turn left. (To visit Aberaeron Harbour, after a few metres, bear right along Market Street.)

Continue along the road and cross the road bridge over Afon

Walled Garden Llanerchaeron

Aeron. Take a track to have the river on your left, and keep ahead through woodland. Ignore paths leading off and the footbridge spanning the river. On reaching a road, cross with care, and bear left over the bridge.

Turn right along the first road, Bro Allt y Graig, which is the road you walked down earlier. Go ahead along the lane and ignore the path on the left into the wood. Pass some houses and then turn right into a small car park. Ignore a track on the left and go ahead on a path which soon bears left through trees.

Continue beside the river and ignore a footbridge, then pass picnic tables and a bungalow. You will pass an information plaque at the point where the short walk joins the main route. The track is narrow and enclosed as it passes between fields, then it goes through a gate onto a broad track. Cross a level bridge over the river and, on reaching a lane, turn left along it to the start of the walk at the car park.

Welsh Cob Stallion Sculpture

OTHER POINTS OF INTEREST

St Non's Church. The present church dates from 1798, but it was substantially altered in the 19th century. The east stained glass window dates from the 1950s and depicts Christ, St David and St Non. Below the church is the Lewis family vault.

Aberaeron Branch Railway. Completed in 1911, the 13 mile branch railway linked Aberaeron with Lampeter, which was on the Aberystwyth to Carmarthen line. There was a halt at Llanerchaeron and several other small places. It closed to passengers in 1951, but milk trains ran from Lampeter to the

Felin Fach creamery until 1973.

Aberaeron. This attractive town was a small fishing hamlet before the harbour was built in the early 18th century. Reverend Thomas Alban Jones Gwynne, a local landowner, perceived the area's potential and promoted a bill through Parliament, resulting in the Harbour Act of 1807. After the harbour, with its stone piers and quays, was completed in 1811, Aberaeron became a busy port exporting cattle , wool and butter. Herring fishing was an important industry, and there were several shipbuilding yards on the south side of the harbour, specialising in schooners and sloops.

Aberaeron, with its wide streets and Georgian to early Victorian houses, is a fine example of early 19th century urban planning. John Nash is reputed to have influenced the plan, but most of the houses were built after his death in 1835. The shipping trade has since declined, but the picturesque town and harbour attract many visitors.

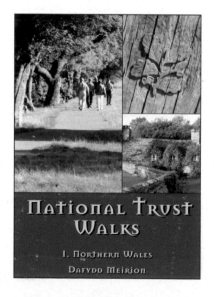